Even So, Joy

*Our Journey through Heartbreak,
Hope, and Triumph*

LESA BRACKBILL

WESTBOW
PRESS®
A DIVISION OF THOMAS NELSON
& ZONDERVAN

Copyright © 2018 by Lesa Brackbill.

All rights reserved. No part of this book may be used or reproduced by any means, graphic, electronic, or mechanical, including photocopying, recording, taping or by any information storage retrieval system without the written permission of the author except in the case of brief quotations embodied in critical articles and reviews.

This book is a work of non-fiction. Unless otherwise noted, the author and the publisher make no explicit guarantees as to the accuracy of the information contained in this book and in some cases, names of people and places have been altered to protect their privacy.

Scripture quotations marked (NIV) are taken from the Holy Bible, New International Version®, NIV®. Copyright © 1973, 1978, 1984, 2011 by Biblica, Inc.™ Used by permission of Zondervan. All rights reserved worldwide. www.zondervan.com The "NIV" and "New International Version" are trademarks registered in the United States Patent and Trademark Office by Biblica, Inc.™

Scripture quotations are taken from the Holy Bible, New Living Translation, copyright ©1996, 2004, 2007, 2013, 2015 by Tyndale House Foundation. Used by permission of Tyndale House Publishers, Inc., Carol Stream, Illinois 60188. All rights reserved.

Cover photo by Alexis LeClair Photography

WestBow Press books may be ordered through booksellers or by contacting:

WestBow Press
A Division of Thomas Nelson & Zondervan
1663 Liberty Drive
Bloomington, IN 47403
www.westbowpress.com
1 (866) 928-1240

Because of the dynamic nature of the Internet, any web addresses or links contained in this book may have changed since publication and may no longer be valid. The views expressed in this work are solely those of the author and do not necessarily reflect the views of the publisher, and the publisher hereby disclaims any responsibility for them.

ISBN: 978-1-9736-1242-1 (sc)
ISBN: 978-1-9736-1241-4 (hc)
ISBN: 978-1-9736-1243-8 (e)

Library of Congress Control Number: 2017919539

Print information available on the last page.

WestBow Press rev. date: 01/30/2018

For Tori

And for all the other Krabbe and leukodystrophy babies
who went to heaven far before their time.
Your strength and courage are why we continue to fight
for universal newborn screening for Krabbe.

A portion of this book's proceeds will be donated to Hunter's Hope.

Contents

Acknowledgments

First and foremost, thank You, God, for opening these doors to tell this story of Your faithfulness and love. Thank You for giving Tori to us and allowing us to be her parents.

Brennan, I love you and am so thankful for you. Thank you for supporting my dreams so selflessly and for being an incredible husband and father. Watching you with Tori brought such joy to my heart, and I cannot imagine living this life with anyone else. As our genetic mutations clearly show, we were meant to be.

Thank you to our parents and family, for being completely supportive throughout our journey. To my parents for sacrificing so much so that you could help us, and for spending months out here serving us. To Amy for your faithful Thursday-night visits and for being so present throughout our journey. To Cheyenne for so selflessly helping us however you could.

To Kristin Roth for giving me the courage to start this in the first place and for editing it—what a gift. I'm so thankful for how God brought us together!

To our church family, Transcend Church Harrisburg, for your love and grace through it all.

To John Neal and Team Krabbe Strong—you do so much for all of us and we thank you.

To Dr. Maria Escolar and her amazing staff members, Barbie, Tara, and Mary.

To Penn State Milton S. Hershey Medical Center and Tori's team of specialists, especially Dr. Debra Byler, Dr. Amanda Ely, and Dr. Faliye. Thank you for your love and compassion, and thank you for respecting Brennan and I and the knowledge we brought to the table. Thank you, also, for being the first hospital (and currently the only hospital) in the state of Pennsylvania to screen all babies born at your hospital for Krabbe.

To the Hummingbird Program, especially Nicole—your support and expertise in palliative care was invaluable, and we are so grateful.

To our leukodystrophy family for their support, love, and acceptance. We would all trade this family for a healthy child, but since we can't change our circumstances, we embrace this special family and love each other.

To Hospice of Central Pennsylvania, especially our nurse, Jenny, for your thoughtful care of Tori and for handling all the necessary tasks after she went to heaven.

To the Quinn Madeleine Foundation—thank you for sending us to Disney World as part of Tori's bucket list. I'm so thankful for the legacy you have established for your Quinn and the families you are helping in her honor.

To the Finley Project—thank you for the support you provided after Tori went to heaven. Your Finley has quite a legacy and would be so proud of how you are helping families.

To the Hunter's Hope Foundation, Judson's Legacy, and the Jackson Project—I cannot say enough about how much we love what you do. Thank you for loving us.

To Early Intervention—Rose, Cheryl, Kelly, Diane, Erica, Tara, and Colleen—thank you for making my weeks brighter and for providing ways to care for Tori that were innovative and stress-relieving. Your visits were a bright spot for me.

To those in the media who loved Tori and helped make her story known, specifically Brant Hansen, Kyle Rogers, Donna Kirker-Morgan: thank you for all that you did for her and for us.

To Representative Angel Cruz and his wonderful staff, Ashley McCahan and Rachel Romanofsky, for continuing to fight for newborn screening for Krabbe in Pennsylvania and for being such an encouragement. Thank you for continuing to include me!

To everyone who brought me coffee or a meal during the day; to Michelle Morrison who was our "chauffeur" to appointments when it became impossible to drive Tori by myself due to her constant need for suctioning; to everyone who sent us cards and gifts for Tori—thank you all for loving us in such tangible, visible ways.

To those who provided extra support consistently: Molly Howard, Karen Schlott, Brian and Kristin Piarulli, Shannon Thornton, Sarah Mae, Amy Smoker, Ashleigh Lindsey, Rachel Gunsauls, Jessica Spangler, Kathy

Kramer, Shian Wing, and many more. Thank you to my Dreamers & Builders friends for your support, encouragement, love, and grace.

Thank you to the team at WestBow Press who made this all happen, and to my faithful launch team for helping spread the word about Tori's story!

Last but certainly not least, Team Tori: this journey would have been much bumpier had it not been for Team Tori and your incredible love, encouragement, support, and hope. Thank you for loving our Tori and for always being there.

Foreword

I saw a big event on YouTube the other day.

All the important people were there. Celebrities. The big stars. Headliners. And they were all gathered together to say something about a tragedy.

There had been a terrorist attack at a concert weeks earlier, and this event was to remember the dead, talk about the attack, and raise money for the victims' families. All worthy reasons to gather, of course. But that wasn't the striking thing about the event.

The striking thing was how little they actually had to say.

They talked of love, and how it's stronger than hate, and I certainly agree with that. But I couldn't help but notice that they were surrounded by such a high level of armed security—helicopters, soldiers, and the like—that the press called it a "ring of steel."

So maybe love is stronger than hate—we can overcome fear, provided love has a little boost from ample firepower and bomb-sniffing dogs. Maybe that's the lesson. I don't know.

And they concluded the event with a tearful rendition of "Somewhere over the Rainbow." Fair enough. But I admit I wanted more. There's got to be more than an unanswered question about bluebirds and rainbows.

I guess I wanted to hear that there's a purpose for the world, and this isn't how the world was supposed to be. That there really is a hope. That things will be set right. That there's a love that transcends even death.

And that death isn't the last and final word.

I'm a skeptic by nature (maybe you can tell), but I'm an equal-opportunity skeptic. I've grown up around American church culture, and I've questioned it at every turn. I've also been exposed to a culture of disbelief, or of vague spiritualities that offer No One transcendent beyond ourselves, and I question that, too.

I want a worldview that makes sense at the funeral of a child.

One that acknowledges the precious value of every human being, no matter what.

One that says, "This is NOT the way it's supposed to be," and then says, "but this is not the last word."

There is unspeakable tragedy in the world. That we know. Now, where do we go with it?

"But how could a loving, all-powerful God allow this sort of thing to happen?" Great question. And here's another one: How arrogant must I be to think that if I can't come up with a reason, a reason can't exist?

If God is real, if the biblical narrative is true, then we know this: God feels our pain. He understands it. He's been through it Himself. And He's going to set things right.

Death wasn't the original plan.

And the Brackbills will see Tori again. The real Tori. Tori made whole.

I didn't become a believer in Jesus because of the Brackbills' story. I was already there. But the Brackbills' story is the reason I'm a believer.

I hope that makes sense.

I read this book, and I remember that in a world full of religious words dressed in lace, of hypocrisies and histrionics, preaching and poses and promises, there yet exists an unshakable reality that can comfort a heartbroken mommy and daddy, and even bring life out of death.

I'm glad I got to meet baby Tori.

I'm even more glad I'll get to meet her again.

—Brant Hansen
storyteller for CURE International, author of *Unoffendable* and
Blessed Are the Misfits, and radio host of *The Brant Hansen Show*

Preface

When the neurologist came in to talk to us, we knew it was bad. You could see it in her eyes. She was dressed in plain clothes, not her typical white doctor's coat. She wasn't supposed to be at work that day. She was somber and unsmiling. All of this was a recipe for disaster.

She shook our hands and then said the most terrible words we could have heard:

"It's Krabbe."

We knew this meant certain death.

It's amazing how one word can transform you in an instant.

Stories are supposed to go a certain way, or so we're told.

You're supposed to grow up, get an education, obtain your dream job, meet the love of your life, get married, have children, and live happily ever after.

So far, ours hasn't gone according to plan.

Tori's story has been unlikely from the beginning.

From the likelihood of Brennan and I meeting to the slight difficulty we had in conceiving her, to the rare genetic disease she inherited and the impact she has had around the world—all of these things could have been marked "unlikely," and yet they all happened.

We have no doubt that Victoria was given to us for a reason, that she was here on this earth for a great purpose. That purpose has yet to be fully revealed to us, but we walk daily in the hope that God is going to redeem our sorrow.

When I started writing our story, I wasn't sure exactly how to frame it, because I don't know what you, the reader, need to get out of it. But the Lord does.

Sadly, I know that we won't be the last couple to lose a child to an impossible situation. Because of that, I wanted to share God's faithfulness and how He helped us through the most terrible time of our lives. But I didn't want to make this a how-to book on getting through the loss of a child, because we are all different and our journeys are unique. If you have lost a child or are in the middle of losing one, I can't tell you how to grieve or how not to grieve. Just because you don't cry every second of every day doesn't mean that you don't love your child fiercely and abundantly. I can't tell you how you will get through it, but I can point you to the One who will be with you every step of the way.

Throughout the book you will see songs mentioned, songs that helped us (and continue to help us) during the events of each chapter. I'm calling it "Background Music"—special thanks to Shannon Thornton for helping me come up with that name! I encourage you to listen to the songs at some point if you don't already know them, and even if you do. I want this book to be as if you were in my living room, listening to me tell Tori's story, with these songs gently playing in the background. Music is a vital part of my life and it has certainly brought untold comfort to my soul.

So, here is our story—God's story, really—about how we met, fell in love, had a baby, discovered her terminal diagnosis, sent her into the arms of Jesus far too soon, and the lessons we learned along the way.

It is our prayer that Tori's life will be an encouragement to you—whether you are also facing a terminal diagnosis for your child, are a parent of healthy children, or are neither of these. The impact of her life is universal, and everyone can learn something from it.

God is good, God is sovereign, and God is faithful. Always.

1 *From California to Pennsylvania*

Background Music:
"You Can Have Me," by Sidewalk Prophets

As long as we have teachable hearts and minds, nothing we experience can be considered a failure or a waste of time.
—ROBERT TURNER

I stepped off the airplane onto the Jetway and could feel the heavy, humid air as I walked to the terminal. The air was stifling, and I wondered if the rest of the summer would feel like this (and how I would survive it). Each step was filled with anticipation as I made my way to the baggage claim, waiting to meet whoever was there waiting for me. It was the beginning of a summer of ministry, a ministry for which I didn't feel prepared but also one to which I knew I had been called.

I was a young California girl in Pennsylvania. I had never planned to go there, nor did I ever expect to do youth ministry. It was my first lesson in trusting God fully and watching Him work, even though I couldn't see His plan at the outset.

♡

My journey to Pennsylvania began as a child, though I didn't know it then.

I was raised in church and became a follower of Jesus around age eight. Jesus has been the most important influence in my life, and I can't remember a time when I didn't know who God was. I am thankful for my godly heritage, because it provides a firm foundation for anything that life brings my way.

Each summer my church would benefit from the service of "summer missionaries," participants in a collegiate program of the Southern Baptist Convention's North American Mission Board in which college students spend ten weeks of their summer doing ministry around the United States. Ours were always from the South, and I knew even as a child that I wanted to be a summer missionary when I was in college. The impact those students had on my life has been lasting, and I will never forget them—in fact, I can still remember many of them by name: Joy, Amanda, Brittany, Robin, Tim, Matt, Barbie.

Fast-forward to 2002, the spring semester of my freshman year at Azusa Pacific University. My friends were all making summer plans, and I decided to apply to be a summer missionary. I wrote down my top three ministry locations—resort ministry being my first choice—and anxiously awaited the North American Mission Board's decision.

I was accepted! But I wasn't going to be serving at a resort on the beach—I was being sent to Central Pennsylvania. Rural, seemingly unexciting Pennsylvania. I admittedly knew nothing about Pennsylvania apart from its rich Colonial and Civil War history, and I was convinced that I was about to have the worst summer ever. This was further cemented in my mind as my friends said things like, "Aren't they all Amish there?" Of course, that isn't true, but their comments didn't help. Despite my misgivings, though, I was ready to serve wherever the Lord took me, and I trusted that He had a plan.

One of the supervisors met me and a few other summer missionaries at the baggage claim, and we headed west on the Pennsylvania Turnpike toward our orientation site. When we arrived, two of the summer missionaries—Josh and Jon—met our van and greeted us. Upon learning where I was from, Jon said, "I wish they all could be California girls!" referencing the Beach Boys' song. Believe it or not, I had never heard *that* one before, and our friendship began at that moment. The three of us served in different cities but were able to connect many times during the summer and enjoyed the friendship that developed and still exists today.

During the three-day orientation, we learned all about Pennsylvania history and culture and received wise missions teaching. I was amazed at how many products are manufactured in Pennsylvania! Our leader, Robert Turner, instilled within us all an appreciation for this place we were about to call home for three months and taught us lessons that would never leave our hearts. One of the many quotable things he said has remained in my memory to this day: "As long as we have teachable hearts and minds, nothing we experience can be considered a failure or a waste of time." Though I didn't realize it at the time, this piece of wisdom would continue to shape my heart for years to come.

After orientation, we all headed to our respective ministry sites and promised to write letters of encouragement (this was pre-Facebook, so snail mail, phone calls, and maybe texting were all we really had). I headed to Williamsport with my supervisor, Kenton, and began my summer (funnily enough, the power was out my first night there, and we had to use candles, so I felt like we were Amish).

That summer was one of the best of my life, and I fell in love with Pennsylvania and with youth ministry. In fact, I went on to do youth ministry for seven years in Southern California while I was attending Azusa Pacific University and after graduation. My faith in the Lord's plan grew as I served there and watched His hand at work all around me. I returned to the same church in Williamsport the following summer—little did I know, I was only an hour away from my future husband, Brennan.

I spent the fall semester of 2003 studying and interning in DC for former speaker of the house Newt Gingrich and his consulting firm, and my experiences there solidified my desire to return to the East Coast after graduation.

In May 2005, with my bachelor of arts in political science in hand, I began to apply for jobs in DC in hopes that I could start a new life there. In the meantime, I continued to work and do youth ministry in my home state, as well as serve wherever God led me—including Tunisia and the Navajo Nation. But there was a longing in my heart for a new address in a certain state, and I continued to pray that God would open doors.

2 Abraham and Isaac

Background Music:
"Holy Is the Lord," by Andrew Peterson

One of the Bible passages that I loved to teach in my seven years of youth ministry was the story of Abraham and Isaac. It's a great story about obedience and about trusting God even when you can't see the outcome, and the students usually walked away with something new to ponder and, hopefully, apply to their lives.

I tried to instill within the teens a passion for God's Word, and along the way, I taught them to remember that these are stories about real people who actually lived on this earth like we do now. It's so easy to read stories in the Bible and forget that these were real humans with real emotions, because the stories mostly focus on facts and the history of the Israelites, often leaving out descriptive language about the emotions involved. But if we stop and imagine what the people could have felt, the stories take on a whole new depth.

Here's the biblical account from Genesis 22:1–18:

> Some time later, God tested Abraham's faith. "Abraham!" God called.
>
> "Yes," he replied. "Here I am."
>
> "Take your son, your only son—yes, Isaac, whom you love so much—and go to the land of Moriah. Go and sacrifice him as a burnt offering on one of the mountains, which I will show you."

The next morning Abraham got up early. He saddled his donkey and took two of his servants with him, along with his son, Isaac. Then he chopped wood for a fire for a burnt offering and set out for the place God had told him about. On the third day of their journey, Abraham looked up and saw the place in the distance. "Stay here with the donkey," Abraham told the servants. "The boy and I will travel a little farther. We will worship there, and then we will come right back."

So Abraham placed the wood for the burnt offering on Isaac's shoulders, while he himself carried the fire and the knife. As the two of them walked on together, Isaac turned to Abraham and said, "Father?"

"Yes, my son?" Abraham replied.

"We have the fire and the wood," the boy said, "but where is the sheep for the burnt offering?"

"God will provide a sheep for the burnt offering, my son," Abraham answered. And they both walked on together.

When they arrived at the place where God had told him to go, Abraham built an altar and arranged the wood on it. Then he tied his son, Isaac, and laid him on the altar on top of the wood. And Abraham picked up the knife to kill his son as a sacrifice. At that moment the angel of the Lord called to him from heaven, "Abraham! Abraham!"

"Yes," Abraham replied. "Here I am!"

"Don't lay a hand on the boy!" the angel said. "Do not hurt him in any way, for now I know that you truly fear God. You have not withheld from me even your son, your only son."

Then Abraham looked up and saw a ram caught by its horns in a thicket. So he took the ram and sacrificed it as a burnt offering

> *in place of his son. Abraham named the place Yahweh-Yireh (which means "the Lord will provide"). To this day, people still use that name as a proverb: "On the mountain of the Lord it will be provided."*
>
> *Then the angel of the Lord called again to Abraham from heaven. "This is what the Lord says: Because you have obeyed me and have not withheld even your son, your only son, I swear by my own name that I will certainly bless you. I will multiply your descendants beyond number, like the stars in the sky and the sand on the seashore. Your descendants will conquer the cities of their enemies. And through your descendants all the nations of the earth will be blessed—all because you have obeyed me."*

There was a newer song out at the time by Andrew Peterson called "Holy Is the Lord" that added such depth to my perspective of the story. The lyrics tell the account from Abraham's viewpoint, bringing emotion into the passage that very well could have been a reality for Abraham. Take a second and look up the lyrics—they are worth it! Here's one line:

And even though You take him, still I ever will obey . . .

Until I heard the song and pondered the lyrics, I admittedly never imagined that Abraham might have actually had emotion as he was obeying the Lord. It's ridiculous, I know, but because the story is told so factually, it never occurred to me to wonder how it made him *feel*. Of course, the song is merely a speculation of the event, but it reminded me that Abraham was human, that he was asked by God to sacrifice his only son, and that he probably had some doubts along the way, even though he acted in obedience.

Here is Abraham, who has waited his *entire* long life to have a son, and God miraculously gives him Isaac, just as He had promised. Then, God tells Abraham to sacrifice that very same son through whom He had promised to multiply his descendants (Genesis 21:12: "But God told

Abraham, '. . . Do whatever Sarah tells you, for Isaac is the son through whom your descendants will be counted'").

I can only imagine what Abraham was thinking. If it had been me, I would have questioned God and made sure that I heard Him correctly—because that couldn't be what He really meant, right?

What I came to learn as I studied this passage was that Abraham fully trusted the Lord and knew that if He was calling him to kill his son, there was an even greater plan in store. He believed God's promises and must have assumed that He would raise Isaac from the dead, since He had promised that Isaac was only the beginning of Abraham's descendants.

So, we are told that he got up early—he didn't procrastinate. I have to wonder, though, if his early departure was the result of a poor night of sleep, wondering what God was doing. Can you imagine, especially if you are a parent, waking up your son to take a journey toward an altar where you would be killing him? It wasn't even nearby—it was a three-day walk! What would you talk about along the way? Was Abraham good at hiding his feelings? The tension and emotion inside Abraham's heart must have been intense.

And yet, he still trusted the Lord with all of his heart and knew that His plans were best.

In verse 5, Abraham tells his servants that both he *and* Isaac would be right back. Whether that was denial, making sure that Isaac felt secure, or simple confidence in the Lord's plan, I'm not sure. Nonetheless, he conveyed his trust in the Lord through his words.

Abraham was obedient even when he didn't understand God's request, and he trusted Him. And the Lord provided a ram at just the right moment. I can almost hear Abraham exhaling a huge sigh of relief when he heard the voice of the angel. I imagine that Abraham's voice was filled with excitement as he lifted scared, confused Isaac up from the altar, embraced him, and told him everything that had happened.

God is always faithful and keeps His promises!

> *It was by faith that Abraham offered Isaac as a sacrifice when God was testing him. Abraham, who had received God's promises, was ready to sacrifice his only son, Isaac, even though God had told him, "Isaac is the son through whom your descendants will be counted." Abraham reasoned that if Isaac died, God was able to bring him back to life again. And in a sense, Abraham did receive his son back from the dead. (Hebrews 11:17–19)*

When I taught on this passage of Scripture, I would play the song I mentioned earlier at some point during the discussion and ask the students to pay attention to the lyrics. I loved hearing their perspectives on it all. Their notions weren't always deep—these were teenagers, after all—but they were always entertaining and often insightful. What a powerful passage and example for us to follow as we walk where the Lord leads.

And even though You take him, still I ever will obey . . .

I would end this lesson by asking the students to look at their own hearts and determine what their "even though" might be. If God were to change something in their lives right then, would they still be obedient? Would they still follow Him and trust His promises? Would I?

3 Make Me Uncomfortable

Background Music:
"Dear Younger Me," by MercyMe

*Through discomfort, I've learned to depend on God when my
natural instinct is to rely on my own skills and talents.*
—Seth Barnes, *Kingdom Journeys*

The greatest lessons in life are learned through discomfort. We see this throughout the Bible: no one grows that much during periods of comfort and prosperity, but they grow exponentially through times of adversity and trials. Look at Moses, Abraham, Joseph, and David, to name a few: the lives of these men did not go as they had anticipated, but God used them in extraordinary ways because of their obedience and willingness to journey without a map in front of them.

We live in a culture that is consumed with convenience and comfort, so we are conditioned to desire those things above all else. This mentality has crept into the church and has affected many Christians along the way. Somehow we have decided that life should be easy, and when it isn't, it can be enough to drive someone away from God.

In December 2007, I began to pray what many considered to be a "crazy" prayer, but it is the prayer that has shaped me to this day in ways I could not have imagined.

I prayed that God would make me uncomfortable.

I was in a spiritual rut and I saw no escape. My faith had grown stagnant and I was desperate for a change. I began to see a pattern in the Bible of growth following discomfort, so I boldly asked God for the same blessing. Had I known what was to come, I might not have prayed so boldly.

> *You can't be remade until you first allow yourself to be unmade.*
> —SETH BARNES, *KINGDOM JOURNEYS*

That year brought so much change in my life. Among all of the other things God allowed that year, I also developed pneumonia (I was told it was just severe allergies at first), which I battled for thirteen weeks. I was extremely sick and lost the ability to sing during that time because my throat was so raw and my lungs were so weak (not to mention that I also tore tissue between my ribs from coughing so violently, so everything I did caused pain). Singing is possibly my greatest God-given talent, so to have it taken away was most definitely uncomfortable. Those weeks were humbling and forced me to rest much more than usual. That period of rest provided time to reflect, time to pray, time to be renewed.

In addition to allowing sickness, He also began to shift relationships in my life and began paving the way for a greater future than I had imagined. In many ways, I felt broken inside, but I remained open to whatever He had for me.

God began to break me so that I could be remade, and it came in ways I never would have anticipated—like moving across the country with no job, only two friends in the area, and a lot of unknowns.

> *Tell God you are ready to be offered, and God will prove*
> *Himself to be all you ever dreamed He would be.*
> —OSWALD CHAMBERS

The move began to take shape in October 2007, during a two-week visit to Pennsylvania. I flew out to sing at my friend Jon's wedding and to attend another friend's wedding the week after. I decided to take a road trip around Pennsylvania to see some of the "kids" who were in my youth group in Williamsport at their respective colleges. As I drove back to Williamsport after spending a few days in Pittsburgh, I was enamored with the fall foliage and the beauty that surrounded me. It hit me strongly that I did not want to return to Southern California.

I'm a California girl, through and through: I lived in Northern California until I graduated from high school, and then I moved to Southern California to attend Azusa Pacific University. By the time I prayed to be uncomfortable, I had already been in Southern California two years longer than I had expected (i.e., I had planned to move right after college), and I felt dread at the thought of returning. My heart yearned for a new start in Pennsylvania.

So, on that beautiful fall day, I pulled the car over with tears in my eyes and began to pray that God would let me move to Pennsylvania. I prayed and prayed . . . and during the next six months I watched God in amazement as He paved the way for the biggest move of my life.

Church became uncomfortable in many ways. I had been serving as the missions coordinator at my church, and a few projects that God had laid on my heart hit a roadblock—unexpectedly, the pastor.

No church is perfect, and no person is perfect, but this pastor in particular seemed to fight any idea that was new or that would change things at the church in any way. The church council loved my idea: I had proposed a detailed plan to have it ready and operating in a short period of time, *and* I had ways to have it completely funded by an outside organization. But the pastor remained firm in his unfounded opposition. This only furthered my frustration and cemented the realization that it was time to pray about how to further God's Kingdom in our community and to be obedient to Him and the ideas He had given me, even if it meant making changes in my life.

Our housing situation became uncomfortable. Very long story short, there were five of us girls (all quiet, college-educated, employed young women) renting a house together in a gated community, and the self-proclaimed leaders of the homeowners association didn't want us there. They wouldn't even let us use the pool. The battle was long and it was irrational, as we were quiet, respectful tenants who truly did not deserve this treatment.

Work became uncomfortable. I had been interviewing for a promotion, and it seemed like it was "in the bag"—we all knew I was going to get it. But I didn't. Someone opted to take a step down (including a pay cut) from a supervisor position to the team leader position that I had worked so hard to achieve. That doesn't just happen. I kept praying.

People need pain to grow. So much of spiritual maturity has to do
with how we process pain. Discipline entails embracing the painful
or unpleasant in the short-term in order to realize long-term gains.
—SETH BARNES, *KINGDOM JOURNEYS*

I was preparing to spend a month in New Orleans with the mission team that I was coleading from Azusa Pacific University, and my company informed me in early March that I would not be allowed to take the time off (even though they had previously approved it). I kept praying, but I knew that this was a *clear* sign. He had led me to colead this team with my friend Holland and He had orchestrated everything (including all of our funding). I knew New Orleans had to happen, and I knew that I would have to quit my job in order to go. And quitting my job meant that I was free to leave Southern California.

On March 18, 2008, God gave me permission to move to Pennsylvania. I was praying as I walked around my neighborhood and I finally got my "verbal" (as opposed to circumstantial) answer: go or stay. He made it clear that He would use me in Southern California and He would use me in Pennsylvania—it was my decision to make. That was a huge lesson in itself, realizing that sometimes God allows us to make decisions and that sometimes there is no "right" answer. My decision was obvious! I was moving to Pennsylvania!

We can't be fully transformed in our own backyard. We need to journey.
—SETH BARNES, *KINGDOM JOURNEYS*

Two weeks after we returned to Southern California from New Orleans, I set out on the biggest adventure of my life thus far. On July 15, 2008, I left Glendora, California, and began the drive to Pennsylvania, having no idea what God really had planned.

I drove away from the life I had known for seven years—and the state in which I had resided my entire life. My mom and I headed east with maps in hand (this was pre-GPS for us) and a great adventure in store.

Yet the biggest adventure awaited me at the end of the trip, eight states and three thousand miles later: building a new life in Harrisburg practically from scratch. With no job, no church, and only a few friends in the area, I trusted the Lord and took the first step, believing that He would prove Himself faithful.

And the adventure continues.

All of this came after I had spent many months praying for the Lord to make me uncomfortable—for Him to present situations that would create both interpersonal growth and growth in my relationship with Him . . . and I never dreamed that would mean moving across the country to a relatively unknown place, leaving everything behind. That is sometimes what He requires of us!

I am so glad that He answered my prayers for discomfort, because the joy that has come from these experiences and from my deepened walk with Him is immeasurable. God is faithful, and when we listen to His voice, we are blessed beyond compare, even when the blessings aren't immediately apparent.

I began life anew in Harrisburg—where I assumed I was destined for a life in Pennsylvania politics. I worked through a temp agency until I landed a position as a junior associate for a lobbying firm in October—the career I had dreamed of for so long. I found a great church quickly and began serving on the worship team (guitar and vocals) and also started a singles' ministry after observing that there were only studies for youth and for married couples.

My life in Pennsylvania was off to an incredible and promising start—but my adventure had only just begun.

4 Brennan

Background Music:
"Then," by Brad Paisley

Brennan was born and raised in a little Pennsylvania town in Juniata County called Mifflintown. His parents divorced when he was only five, and his dad's parents helped raise him because his dad worked long hours to provide for his children and his mom lived nearly an hour away.

He was always a "good kid" and rarely got into trouble. He was a protector of his siblings, Jared and Kelly, and watched out for them at every opportunity. I asked his mom, Amy, for examples, and these were two of my favorites:

> Brennan and his brother didn't have school on Columbus Day, so Jared and he were on Licking Creek Road riding bikes when Jared's tire went off the berm of the road, sending him over the handlebars, and he hit the macadam with his face, cracking both sides of his jaw. Brennan did not freak out but instead tore his shirt off to wrap around Jared's injuries and went for help.
>
> Then, there was the time when I lived in Steelton and Brennan was watching Jared and Kelly for me while I worked a few hours on a Saturday morning. I got home and he said that everything was great. It was months later, at an open house at his school, that I discovered a story hanging on the wall in one of his classes. The story proceeded to inform everyone that Jared and Kelly wanted chocolate syrup, which I did not

have, so Brennan decided to melt Hershey's Kisses in the microwave, which exploded everywhere and made a big mess. He did a fine job cleaning up because I never had a clue!

Brennan was blessed by his grandparents' value system of respect, responsibility, working hard, and following the Lord. In a similar way, he was challenged to live a good life by watching his parents' lives before they came to know Jesus. They were open about their mistakes and he chose to learn from them instead of repeat them.

He was athletic (volleyball, track, baseball, hockey), musical (trumpet and vocals), and intelligent. Brennan did whatever he could to help those around him and was known for his reliability.

His godly grandparents took him to church faithfully, but it wasn't until he attended Creation Northeast (a large, multiday Christian music festival in central Pennsylvania) that he accepted Jesus as his Lord and Savior at the age of fifteen. Brennan remembers that night vividly, down to the specifics of the message he heard: the pastor spoke about accepting responsibility for your life and your faith, that you may fail but God never will, and that His will may not be exactly what you want or plan on, but it's always best for you.

After high school, Brennan became involved with a local Christian camp (Christian Retreat Center) as a counselor, assistant program director, and paintball camp director for many years. We are still involved with this camp today and love seeing lives changed by Jesus. His best friend, Jeremy Kerstetter, was the program director at the time, and he told me a funny story about those early CRC days:

When Brennan first started working at CRC, he went through counselor training and at the end, he told me that he didn't really have patience for kids. Not the words you want to hear from your counselor, but he was willing. The first several weeks, he needed to take a walk several times, but after the first year, his commitment to ministering at CRC was unrivaled.

Brennan attended Penn State and graduated in 2000 with a degree in kinesiology and athletic training. He wasn't sure exactly what he wanted to do with his degree, but he found a passion for massage therapy and pursued that as a career. He attended massage therapy school while continuing to deliver pizzas in his hometown.

Once he had completed his massage therapy certificate, he was hired at The Spa at The Hotel Hershey—possibly the best spa in Pennsylvania—in 2003, and he still works there today.

With this amazing opportunity in hand, he began his new life in Hershey and purchased a condo so that he would no longer have to commute an hour each way. He became a season-ticket holder for the Hershey Bears, found a church he enjoyed attending, and made many new friends.

In 2009, his church was going through a rough time and eventually split, so when his mom invited him to go to church with her at East Shore Baptist on Easter, he readily accepted the invitation.

He had no idea that he was about to meet his future wife.

5 Easter Sunday 2009

**Background Music:
"We Won't Be Shaken," by Building 429**

She brings him good, not harm, all the days of her life.
—PROVERBS 31:12

For years I wondered whether or not I would ever get married, whether or not that was truly God's plan for my life. From early on, I had decided to let God write my love story (after reading a book called *When God Writes Your Love Story* by Eric and Leslie Ludy), because I learned the hard way that Satan likes to use boys to hurt girls emotionally (and vice versa, of course), and I am still dealing with some of those scars today. I rarely "dated" boys as a result of my experiences and my decision to let God be in control, and I was truly content for a majority of my college career—until all my friends started getting married.

As I attended wedding after wedding and watched my closest friends move into a new phase of life (one that I deeply desired), I made a decision to follow and trust the Lord instead of worrying and stressing—figuring that He knows me better than I know myself, and knowing that life is better when we do things His way. The woman described in Proverbs 31:12 brought good, not harm, to her husband *all* the days of her life—which means even before she knew him! What a challenge that verse presented me! But I determined to do my best to achieve that goal.

When God led me to move to Pennsylvania, many people asked me if it was for a guy. I honestly was able to say no . . . . But of course, a hope existed in my heart that I would meet my "Prince Charming" and finally find true love. I moved, began to build friendships, went on a few blind dates (most of which were laughably terrible), and found an incredible church. It was in this church that I began to find my "place" in Pennsylvania. This is where God called me in 2002 and 2003 to serve, and this is where He called me in 2008 to live. I started a singles' ministry at my church, as it was truly needed (the irony is that I met my husband one week before the class started). That same month, I became part of a team that would plant a church in Harrisburg that fall. God was clearly using my talents and abilities for His purposes and glory, and I was so content!

I began to realize that my singleness all those years was never a mistake—I was able to devote so much time to serving the Lord without distraction, including the ability to lead the monthlong mission trip to New Orleans and fully devote myself to our mission there. Had I been in a relationship, those things would have been much more difficult. God had specific plans for me through all my years of singleness, and I don't regret a single moment!

Sometimes I wish God would clue us in when we're unknowingly experiencing a moment that we'd want to remember vividly forever. A little nudge would be amazing.

My best example: when I met Brennan. That was a slightly important moment in my life, and I honestly don't remember much about it. Neither does he.

It was on Easter Sunday, April 12, 2009, around noon. It was at East Shore Baptist Church. My life was about to change and I was clueless.

I remember that I had been up since 4:00 a.m. My church offered three services on Easter instead of their typical two, and as the guitarist / lead female vocalist, I was asked to help lead all three services. This meant a 4:00 a.m. wake-up call, a 5:00 a.m. warm-up time, and a very long—but good—day. I was looking forward to the time of worship and celebration of our Lord's resurrection from the dead. I knew that it would be tiring and that my voice would be exhausted after all that singing. I knew what to expect from the day. I had no idea that I was about to meet the love of my life.

By the time the third service was over, I was exhausted. I remember that Brennan's mom—whom I had known for a few months by this point, though I didn't know she had a son named Brennan—said something about wanting me to meet someone and that I (the exhausted introvert) reluctantly agreed. She introduced me to her very tall son, Brennan, and we shook hands. I invited him to join us the following week at our new Bible study for young single adults, and that was about it.

Why is it that we can often remember the boring, trivial details about such important moments, but not the details that really matter? Why can't I remember what he said, how he looked at me?

I wasn't looking for love that day, or even a date. But God, in His sovereignty and grace, took that uneventful first meeting and turned it into a lifelong love.

Brennan will tell you that I was "grumpy" that day (but what he really means is that I wasn't very talkative). But like me, he doesn't really remember any first impressions or much about that meeting because it was so laughably unmemorable.

It was through that Bible study that we got to know each other and our friendship developed. I had been in a car accident six months prior, so when I found out that he was a massage therapist, I quickly struck a deal with him wherein I would feed him dinner if he would work on my neck and shoulders. The first massage was only supposed to last thirty minutes, but we were talking and having a nice conversation, so thirty minutes became nearly an hour.

About six weeks later I found out that he had a cold, so I took soup to his condo and set it on the porch. I figured I would hear from him relatively quickly, but no text came. I waited and waited and finally texted him to see if he would mention the soup. He didn't at first, so I finally told him what I had done and warned him that, by that time, it had been sitting out for hours so he shouldn't eat it. He laughed. It turns out his roommate had put the soup in the fridge for him so it was safe.

A month or so later, after we had been texting frequently for a week or two, I invited him to come to a movie in the park with a group of us from church. *Kung Fu Panda* was the feature of the evening, and we watched it as fireflies danced around us. Nothing special happened that night, but I went home and wrote in my journal that I had met the man I was going to marry. Somehow, I just knew. Thankfully, he shared my interest and we started dating a few days later.

We were friends for three months, dated for six, were engaged for nine, and have been happily married since November 6, 2010.

Brennan completely caught me off guard me with the timing of his proposal—January 27, 2010—and he was so happy that he succeeded, because I'm not easy to surprise. The impending proposal was not unanticipated, as we had decided in August that we were heading toward marriage and he had asked my dad's permission to marry me at Christmas. The timing, however, was unexpected.

He wanted to propose at our church, right where we first met. As we were taking off our coats that Wednesday evening so that I could practice for an upcoming concert, I heard him say, "Shoot! You know what?" When I turned around, he had a ring box in his hand and was preparing to get down on one knee. I was so surprised, because I wasn't expecting the proposal for another month or two.

We were engaged! We set the date for November 6, 2010, and prepared for a Northern California wedding. It was a perfect day, warm and sunny. We couldn't have asked for better weather or a more perfect celebration with so many of our loved ones in attendance.

I kept one secret from Brennan until ten days before our wedding, but it was for a good reason. In 2002, while sitting on a porch in Williamsport, Pennsylvania, I began writing letters to my future husband in a little journal, not knowing that he was so close to me geographically. I wrote with the intent of giving it to my future husband right before my wedding. This journal contains great memories and many special notes, including one entry on July 14 (five days before we officially started dating) that simply said that I knew I was going to marry him—because I did! I kept a timeline and notes about our relationship, things that we will laugh about in the future and will want to remember for years.

I gave that journal to Brennan the day before I left for California (for our wedding) and was so excited for him to read my prayers for him, for us, and all the other treasures those letters contain. Eight years of praying for him, writing to him, most of which before I even knew his name. Eight years of wondering, of searching, of aching for the love that I now know.

Writing those letters helped me maintain my focus on purity and on "not settling" for any guy that came along. Sure, I wondered every time I met a new guy whether he could be "the one," but none really seemed right. And honestly, God really protected me all those years, because it was rare for a guy to express interest in me beyond friendship, even though I had far more male friends than female. My focus remained solid: I sought to know the Lord, to keep myself pure, and to serve Him wherever He led.

Our marriage has been relatively easy and wonderful. Our bond is strong, and that would prove to be necessary in the years to come. Much like the Brad Paisley song we danced to on our wedding day says, "We've come so far since that day, and I thought I loved you then." I never could have imagined how much love grows and deepens almost daily when you are intentional about cultivating your marriage.

I may not remember very clearly the details of when we met, but I am no less thankful for what joy the last eight years (and counting) have brought to my life. I can't imagine living life with anyone but Brennan.

6 A New Perspective

Background Music:
"There Is a Reason," by Alison Krauss & Union Station

In 2001, I was ready to take on the world. I wanted to be the governor of California someday, with every intention of being my friend's vice president in 2028 (we even had a website!). High-profile aspiration is an understatement.

That's how I saw myself: working in politics to change our country for the better, and everyone would know my name and how awesome I was. Let's be honest—I wanted to feel important, to be admired and respected because of my capabilities, talents, and brilliance. In one word, pride.

Over the next few years, I interned with Newt Gingrich in Washington DC, I worked on (and ran) several campaigns, attended the 2005 Presidential Inauguration (and a ball), and was even on ABC for thirty seconds. I attended campaign training at President Reagan's ranch in Santa Barbara and was pictured in *TIME* magazine with the rest of the training group. I was on my way . . . or so I thought.

Fast-forward to 2007: it was two years past graduation and I was still living in Southern California—not my plan. I kept trying to get back to DC, but doors would just not open. Instead, I was working for a financial company fixing tax returns all day long—completely low profile—along with doing youth ministry at my church.

I eventually became content (but not fully happy) in the tax job and even tried to move into management, but to no avail. Even though my bosses said I was the perfect candidate for management, I continued to be passed over for promotions, and it didn't make sense to any of us. But it was a good job, so I remained there.

After moving to Pennsylvania, I worked through a temp agency for a while until obtaining a job with a lobbying firm—which I thought was *perfect*! This was it—my door into the political arena!

Boy, was I wrong. Looking back, I firmly believe that God allowed me to have that position for a year to show me that He did *not* want me in politics like I had planned. It was a terrible year—the job was an awful fit and I was so miserable in that role. I saw a side of politics that I had never seen before and I was completely disillusioned. I was let go in September 2009, and the joy that I felt was indescribable! Most people aren't happy after being fired (or in my case, "forced to quit"), but all the heaviness that had weighed on my heart disappeared, and I felt so free. I am thankful for the experience that job gave me, but it was time to move on.

From there, I was unemployed for nearly a year, and that year was an incredible gift to me. I watched as God provided faithfully for me and I was able to pay my rent until April 2010 (through some unconventional ways, the most memorable being when Brennan went to Atlantic City with a few of his guy friends and won enough during poker to cover my rent), when I moved in with Brennan's aunt and uncle until our wedding. I was able to focus on church planting and mission trips (to Haiti and Brazil), and I was so filled with joy. God's provision was constant, and though it was a humbling year, I learned to accept help from others and to not be proud. I learned more during that year of unemployment than I thought possible—lessons that have proven to be invaluable even today.

While it took me a while to realize this, there's a common thread throughout most of the jobs I have held: I was rarely thanked or recognized for my work, and I have never really used my very expensive bachelor's degree. I have had many supervisors—both good and bad—and most made me feel unappreciated.

Working as a relief houseparent at Milton Hershey School (a residential school for impoverished children started by Mr. Milton S. Hershey in 1909 and partially funded by Hershey's Chocolate today—I will discuss this more in a later chapter) is largely a "thankless" job where the students are concerned—students aren't going to thank you for disciplining them, after all. Don't get me wrong—I LOVE it, and it's highly rewarding to help these students make decisions and learn lessons! My point is that they don't care about the fact that I'm intelligent, a great musician/vocalist; they don't really care that I am a good photographer, or that I was once in *TIME* magazine. They just want to be fed (they are middle school boys, after all), entertained, and kept safe. Above all, they want to be loved.

Stick with me—there is a point to all of this. God used my job experiences to reveal some things to me and to change my heart about my future in a major way.

One day, as I was talking with a dear friend about her potential job opportunities (very prestigious and impressive jobs for which she was perfectly suited), all of the aforementioned things started to run through my head. As I listened to her speak, I realized that I, too, longed to be admired for what I could do—for my God-given gifts and abilities, for what I worked so hard to accomplish in college/postcollege. I longed to be known as someone who "did something" with her life, whatever that even means. I, too, tended to put my value and self-worth in my career, in how people viewed me, and what I'd done, which explained so much about why I had felt so miserable in recent jobs. That hasn't changed since 2001.

But you know what did change? In 2013 my desire to be a mother (a stay-at-home one, at that) increased exponentially—considering that I never saw myself doing that, it wasn't hard for it to increase drastically. I came to realize that raising children to love Jesus and to be productive members of society is the greatest possible career that I could ever have. What a stark contrast to how I felt even one year before.

It became very clear that God had used the circumstances of the past decade to prepare me for being a mom. Being a mother is often a "thankless" job, as you continuously and often sacrificially serve your children. Someday, they might recognize the amazing job you did taking care of them and preparing them for life, but humans are naturally born selfish. They aren't going to say, "Thanks, Mom, for changing my diaper so that I don't get diaper rash," or, "Thanks, Mom, for staying up all night with me when I was sick"—that's just how it goes. They don't care how accomplished you are and they certainly aren't going to marvel over your talents—at least not for many years.

Being a mother requires humility, sacrifice, unconditional love, and lots of grace . . . and I know now that I am much better equipped for motherhood because of the circumstances of the past sixteen or so years—so much makes sense now. I was in desperate need of humility, and God brought circumstances into my life to teach me how to be humble. I wish I had been a faster learner! Not that I'm completely humble now—I'm definitely not. But given where I was in 2001, I have come a long way and my perspective has completely changed. I was so unaware of the grip that pride was holding on my life!

I now view the word *rewarding* completely differently. To me, it no longer means being recognized and praised—it means offering recognition and praise while expecting nothing in return, all for the benefit of others. So now I have something new to embrace and something hard with which to grapple.

God doesn't want me to be "famous"—He wants me to make disciples, including my own future children. I need to remind myself constantly that it doesn't matter what the world thinks of me or whether they notice how "awesome" I might happen to be.

What matters is that I live my life according to the Gospel, and that I share it with others at every opportunity. What matters is that I find ways to use my God-given gifts and talents to further the Kingdom of God, especially within my own household, without doing it selfishly or for recognition.

What matters are the eternal things, not the temporal. What matters is that my value and self-worth come from God alone and not from anything that I have done or will do.

If you had asked me three years prior to Tori's birth whether I was content not having children, I would have said yes, because I wanted a career. Yet, as I continued to try to find contentment in a career, I continued to become more frustrated, more discontent. I would come home feeling so sad because I just wasn't passionate about what I was doing. Unfortunately, that's the way I am wired—passion is a requirement in order to find fulfillment.

But God changed my perspective on having children and being a stay-at-home mom, and it became my greatest dream. Being a full-time mom uses all of my gifts and abilities in unique ways, and I love it.

We tried to conceive for about a year and a half and were afraid that we were having infertility issues, not knowing that many couples take a couple of years to conceive their first child. Those months were difficult because I knew that I was meant to be a mother and I wanted it so much.

On December 1, 2013, I decided to take a pregnancy test because I was a week late, and it was positive! We were pregnant! The journey of parenthood had only begun.

7 Pregnancy and Victoria Ruth

Background Music:
"Cinderella," by Steven Curtis Chapman

As we walked around Babies "R" Us completing our baby registry, I was overwhelmed by the number of decisions that needed to be made and the amount of "stuff" we were told that we must have in order to care for our baby.

One of the most irritating decisions was the actual theme of her nursery; there were dozens of possibilities, but most were, in my opinion, over the top and borderline obnoxious. Since my pregnancy hormones made me far more irritable than usual, this wasn't a surprising reaction. Brennan, my sister Cheyenne (I lived with her family in Williamsport while serving there, and we decided in 2002 that we were sisters; she is such a blessing to this day), and I walked down aisle after aisle, hoping for inspiration.

As we walked down the sheets aisle, I noticed a set that had maps on it (I love maps and geography) and there were animals on the continents. Right next to these sheets was a blanket with a fuzzy giraffe on it. Maps and giraffes it was!

We didn't choose giraffes because they had some special meaning to us—it was a completely arbitrary decision so that we could check that box on the list and be done. We had no idea how popular giraffes were and how plentiful giraffe-themed items would become. We just wanted to make a decision and move forward to the more important preparations for parenthood: our hearts.

The pregnancy continued normally for the most part, and I loved being pregnant. I loved feeling her move inside of me—and since she was very active, I felt her constantly. I was nervous about becoming a mother, because I've never felt like I was good with children, but I trusted the advice I had heard from so many: it's different when the child is your own.

With the exception of having gestational diabetes (managed by diet alone until the final month of pregnancy) and the fact that Tori loved to sleep through the many "nonstress tests" (thereby making them extremely stressful and necessitating an ultrasound many times a week to prove to the doctor that she was okay), the pregnancy progressed smoothly and my heart became increasingly prepared for motherhood, even though I knew that it would be filled with constant surprises.

Photo by Shannon Thornton Photography

From the moment I knew she was coming, Tori brought pure joy to my heart. Joy deeper and richer than any I had known before. It only multiplied and grew after I first held her and beheld her beauty.

Victoria Ruth entered our world on July 30, 2014, at 9:25 a.m. Eight pounds, seven ounces, and twenty and three-quarter inches long. Black hair and a lot of it (just like her mama). Eyelashes that any woman would envy (just like her daddy). Perfection. I never knew I could love someone so much.

As all parents say, our lives truly changed forever. Little Miss Brackbill made her appearance after fourteen hours of natural labor, six hours of labor with an epidural, and finally, a C-section. Nothing went as we had planned or hoped, but ultimately what mattered was that she was healthy, happy, and here with us.

I was induced at 12:00 p.m. on July 29 at the hospital and then sent home to wait. I began having contractions at home by 1:00 p.m. and my water broke around 3:30 p.m., so we headed back to the hospital where they confirmed that I was indeed in labor and was three centimeters dilated. We were taken to our labor and delivery room around 6:30 p.m., and the "fun" really began there.

I had planned to have a completely natural birth—no medicine or interventions—and I successfully labored for ten hours that way. However, around 11:00 p.m. I decided to ask for pain medication as I was exhausted, hungry, and in so much pain (obviously). I had another dose around 1:00 a.m. and then finally caved and asked for an epidural around 3:00 a.m. I was only six centimeters dilated, and the contractions were getting to be too much for me. I cried when I made that decision, because it was definitely not what I had ever wanted, but I am so glad that I opted to have one—I went from 6 centimeters to 9.5 centimeters in an hour after the epidural was in place! Had my labor been shorter, I think I could have made it naturally . . . but it was just too much.

They allowed me to rest until 6:30 a.m., which was wonderful except for the few moments of fear when I woke up surrounded by nurses who were flipping me over on my side and wouldn't explain what was going on. My blood pressure had dropped and so had Tori's heart rate, apparently, but they were able to resolve that quickly.

Beginning at 6:30 a.m., I pushed for two hours with no success. Finally, at 8:30 a.m., my doctor said that a C-section was necessary because the baby wasn't going to fit through the birth canal. They had suspected early on that my birth canal might be "narrow," but this confirmed the suspicion. TMI, I know.

At this point, I was so exhausted that I welcomed the decision, though I was again disappointed because I hadn't been able to deliver her naturally.

However, Brennan was (as always) a wonderful support and he reminded me that it doesn't matter how she comes out, just that she does.

Tori was born at 9:25 a.m. and I was in recovery by 11:00 a.m. I didn't get to hold her until about an hour after her birth, because my arms were numb from the anesthesia. But Brennan was able to be with her the whole time after birth, following her around as she was weighed and measured, and then doing "skin to skin" time with her since I was unable to do so. While he held her, he sang the song "Cinderella" by Steven Curtis Chapman, not realizing what an impact that song would later have on our lives. I am so thankful for those first couple of days where he was able to be her main caretaker—what a great bonding experience for them!

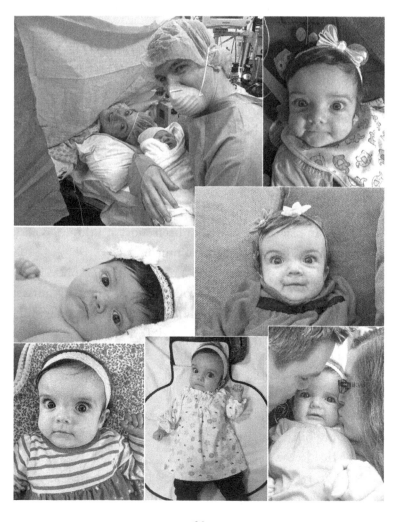

While I was pregnant, we chose to keep her name a secret for many reasons (mostly because we didn't decide on her name until about a month before she was born), and it was such fun to finally reveal it to our family and friends. We chose Victoria because it means "victorious," and we knew that with Jesus she would be victorious.

She didn't officially have a middle name until during labor; we had been deciding between Ruth and Joy. In my exhaustion after such a long labor, I asked Brennan to choose and he chose Ruth. We chose Ruth to honor one of her great-grandmothers—my mom's mom—someone who has been such an incredible part of my life and such a great example of what it means to be a godly woman. We chose to give her a nickname from birth because we love the name Tori, and we wanted her to have a strong full name to really know when she was in trouble.

I was discharged at my request after forty-eight hours, as I was feeling great but also knew that I would rest far better at home. I only took small doses of pain medication for two days at home, and I praise the Lord for a mostly painless recovery. I didn't know beforehand that I wouldn't be allowed to walk up or down stairs, so I was unexpectedly confined to only one floor of our house. I wasn't terribly disappointed, though, because that meant that someone else had to do laundry for two weeks!

My parents, Ken and DeAnne, arrived from California shortly after Tori's birth and stayed with us for eighteen days. They were a tremendous support to Brennan, Tori, and me, and it was so nice to have them here to spend time with their first grandchild.

On our blog, which I had been keeping since 2003, I wrote,

> Tori has adjusted to life on earth fairly well, though we had a few rough and sleepless nights. However, she's learning and so are we, and we just keep reminding ourselves that this will get better, and that these days are precious and numbered. Someday we'll look back and think that this was the easy time in life.

And thus we began our adventure of parenthood and all that it entails. Tori was independent from the start and we loved her feisty personality.

She was a delight—rarely fussy, and even then it was only when she was tired—always smiling, playing, laughing, talking. Always moving!

A couple of weeks after she was born, I remember remarking to Brennan that "no news must be good news" in regard to her newborn screenings—the simple heel-prick test they do in all hospitals to check for many genetic disorders that can be treated if caught early. We didn't know much about the test then, but we took the lack of results to indicate perfect health for our precious baby girl.

Her blue eyes were so big and mesmerizing—like those of a Disney princess. Everyone noticed them and we were enamored with them. Her beautiful eyes were so expressive and photogenic, and I have thousands of pictures of them. I tried not to be "that mom" but I posted them all on social media because I just couldn't help it. Everyone needed to see those eyes!

I was surprised to find that motherhood suited me so much better than I ever dreamed, and it truly brought out the best in me most of the time. Being at home every day as a wife and mother is the most fulfilling thing I have ever done. I can't imagine doing anything else full-time, which is a stark contrast to my previous aspirations.

At her two-month well-check appointment, the pediatrician measured her head a few times to verify the growth that had occurred and requested that we take her for an ultrasound because her head had grown a little too quickly in such a short time. We took her to the hospital for the ultrasound and everything appeared to be normal. In hindsight, this should have been a much bigger red flag than it was.

She grew and developed and her future was so bright. We couldn't believe how amazingly good she was all the time. We flew to California when she was just four months old, and she never cried. She charmed all of the flight attendants and surrounding passengers with her smile and her big eyes. She loved traveling! She was truly joy personified.

Portrait Session by Alexis LeClair Photography

♡

On January 6, 2015, a new headband I had ordered for her online arrived— black with white polka dots—and she looked so adorable in it. I took pictures—like I typically did each day—and posted them for all our family and friends to see. She was extra adorable that day, I remember. What I didn't know then was that our lives were about to change forever, in the blink of an eye.

8 A Week of Lasts and Krabbe at First Sight

Background Music:
"Eye of the Storm," by Ryan Stevenson

Most parents reminisce about their child's firsts—first word, first steps, first everything. It's exciting to watch our children learn and grow as they explore their new world. For Brennan and I, it seems that we remember the lasts much more vividly—always in hindsight. Even now it is hard to pinpoint exactly when she lost certain abilities, because most of them happened so gradually that we didn't even notice; or, we assumed she just wasn't feeling well one day and therefore was not doing normal things, when in actuality she had lost another ability.

I often wonder if the Lord allowed us to have five perfect months with Tori because of what He knew was going to happen. Five months with a perfect baby; five months of smiles, laughter, and joy; five months of calm before the storm. As our Tori lost more and more of her previously achieved milestones in the months to come, we remembered. We mourned. The first week of January 2015 was one of lasts, but we didn't realize it then.

I wrote on our blog about this one year later, in January 2016:

> This week last year marks the last time Tori smiled, laughed, played with her toys, attempted to move on her own, and many other abilities. She rolled over for the first and last time this week last year. And then the number of photos posted daily slows down drastically, indicating that Krabbe came on with full force. She

35

stopped being herself so suddenly and we didn't even realize it at the time.

However, in the midst of the sadness these memories bring, there is also immense joy. Every breath she breathes. Every time she opens her beautiful eyes. Every sigh of contentment. Every day that we are given with her is precious beyond words and we are filled with gratitude. We are thankful for her presence. For how she has impacted our lives and the lives of thousands who follow her story. For how she has changed us for the better.

She has taught us to love abundantly, to live fully, to forgive wholeheartedly, and to show grace freely. We are thankful for our Victoria.

She is such a fighter and we can see her continue to try to fight Krabbe with all she has; she is only on one med now instead of three; her visual perception improved as of last month. She even held her head up by herself two days ago! God gave her to us for a reason, and we will love her for the rest of our lives. We love this baby girl even more than we did one year ago—our love is more fierce, more intentional, more compassionate.

Habakkuk's God is not one who promises safety from the agonies of life; rather, He is a God who is sovereign over the agonies of life. Habakkuk's God does not promise deliverance in the valley of the shadow of death, but presence. He is a God of love more extravagant and resolute than we can imagine.
—HEATHER ZEMPEL, *AMAZED AND CONFUSED*

I've learned several times in my life that if you don't purposely make memories, you will lose them. If you aren't fully present, things will slip away from your memory without your consent. Things like meeting

Brennan—I can tell you the date and place, but that's about it. It didn't seem noteworthy at the time. As a photographer, I make memories through my lenses. It's just how my mind works—I feel more present while I am capturing images than if I were just observing.

Because of this, Tori's life has been well-documented from day one—I sent pics to Brennan at work throughout the day, posted on Facebook for my California family, and so forth. We have thousands of photos of her first five months of life. We can only pinpoint the onset of Krabbe (crab-ay) disease to January 7, 2015, because of the lack of photos taken for days at a time.

In hindsight, we can see Krabbe in Tori as far back as December 19, 2014. In the moment, we had no idea why Tori was so upset. She wouldn't nurse. She seemed so angry that I had the audacity to try to feed her.

This wasn't our Tori.

We couldn't get her to stop this new, terrifying cry no matter what we tried. Now we know that she was in an incredible amount of pain due to the breakdown of the myelin sheath, which is the coating that protects all of the nerves throughout the body—more on that later. She cried and cried, and we felt helpless.

And then she stopped. Our happy girl reappeared. She was fine until we put her in her car seat to go to a surprise birthday party for Brennan's grandfather, and then she was fussy again. Once we arrived, she was back to her charming self and she met many family members for the first time. It would be the only time many of them would see her healthy.

I wish we had known that we should be more concerned. But all the initial symptoms of Krabbe are easily explained away. And once symptoms appear, it is usually too late for a stem-cell transplant, which is currently the best form of treatment. After a round of chemotherapy the baby is given cord blood from an unrelated donor and the body uses the stem-cells to resolve the enzyme deficiency that the Krabbe mutation cause. Without the transplant, death is imminent.

We would have about two more weeks with our healthy Tori before Krabbe would take up full residence in her brain. Our story might be significantly different if only she had been tested at birth, as that is the only opportunity to effectively treat Krabbe and save the child's life.

As I mentioned before, between January 1 and 10 we took hardly any pictures of Tori. It was during those days that Krabbe took over her precious brain and robbed her of her smile, her laugh, her voice (except crying), and many other skills. And we had no idea.

Tori became inconsolable—our previously perfect baby was miserable, and it was admittedly frustrating. Everything was "explainable" according to the books, which said that extreme irritability and loss of milestones could be teething, reflux, or a growth spurt. After all, if a baby doesn't feel well, why would they smile? I tried to ignore my fears, but they were persistent. Something was wrong.

There are ranges for each milestone, and I hadn't worried about the fact that she wasn't even trying to meet some of them yet. But when I started to see friends post photos and videos of their babies, close in age to Tori and some younger than her, achieving milestones that she hadn't yet even attempted, I started to wonder.

I couldn't shower, cook, eat, or anything else without her crying because I wasn't holding her. I didn't think about the possibility that she wasn't feeling well or that she was in pain. This has been my first experience with feeling "mommy guilt," because I had no idea what was really going on.

One day I realized that I hadn't seen her smile or heard her talk in about two weeks; it took me a while to see it—because you rarely notice a change unless it happens for an extended period of time. I joked with Brennan that we must not be funny anymore because she just wasn't laughing or smiling.

I looked back through my videos and the last one of her talking and smiling was on December 29. Since the Internet has answers for everything, I began to research out of desperation. I read that babies will often stop talking when they are working on another milestone or when teething, so I didn't think much about it during those first two weeks. But combined with her other behavior changes, it was time to call the doctor.

When I spoke with her pediatrician, he believed it was reflux—which we would later discover is the most common misdiagnosis of Krabbe.

Brennan and I had just been talking about how she felt heavier, and we were so thrilled to see her growing, since she had been so petite thus far. So when the nurse came to weigh her at our appointment and found that she had only gained two ounces since our last well-check visit, I started to be afraid. My five-month-old weighed only eleven pounds, nine ounces.

The doctor reweighed her to verify the unbelievable number on the scale, and it was accurate. He measured her again to verify the nurse's report and found that her head had continued to grow—which he took to mean that her brain was getting the nutrients it needed even though the body growth had slowed. Her body was now in the second percentile and her head was in the ninety-seventh.

As I described her behavior and symptoms, he suggested that we try reflux medicine, as everything pointed to an acid reflux issue. It appeared that she was only eating enough to get the hunger pains to go away, explaining the lack of weight gain and her frequent feedings. It also explained the rest of the behavior changes so well. He wrote a prescription for baby Zantac and said it could take seven to ten days to take effect and up to two weeks before we'd see a change in behavior. He said if the meds didn't work, he wanted to have an MRI of her head done to address the lack of development and the regression of talking and smiling.

I left the appointment feeling encouraged because the diagnosis made sense, but I still had doubts and found myself worrying that something else was wrong. I never could have imagined the truth. That same day we went to IKEA in Baltimore with a friend, and Tori cried the entire way there and back (an hour and a half each way). I knew then that something was terribly wrong and that it wasn't reflux, but I didn't know what it was.

The next day, she had an upper GI study at the hospital, and everything looked good. Her stomach and intestines were functioning as they should be, which ruled out a few possible diagnoses.

Most of the time, I am not a worrier or a fearful person because I trust the Lord completely. But around day seven of the medicine, with no changes or improvement in behavior, fear began to take over. My brain kept thinking about the what-ifs, the worst possible scenarios. I found myself in tears at one point thinking about losing her to whatever this could be. I had to pray and pray to fight the fearful thoughts in my mind.

One thing that has surprised me about motherhood is the depth of my emotions in regard to my love for Tori. It drove me to prayer more than anything ever has. I combatted the fear with prayer and with truth—that God is sovereign and in control—but also knew I needed to take action.

Around day eight of the reflux medication, I *really* started to question its effectiveness, because she still seemed to be miserable. I also continued to sense that something more was going on. But since she was sleeping a bit better and had been slightly less fussy since we started the meds, I waited it out.

By day thirteen of the reflux medication, I knew I had to make another appointment because things weren't getting better; in fact, things seemed to be getting worse.

We returned to her pediatrician and when he did her measurements again, he found that she had only gained an ounce in two weeks, despite the fact that we had started to introduce solid food at his suggestion. And after listening to my observations and listening to Tori's cries, he became convinced that she was indeed in pain. He thought it was from migraine-like headaches that were possibly being caused by excess fluid in the skull. This would explain her getting upset and then throwing up, too, because she was feeling nauseated. And who wants to learn or try new things with a migraine? It was decided that an MRI was needed, but they were not able to get one scheduled until May 6, 2015.

He said that her symptoms and the possible diagnosis made sense with the jump in her head size that happened at two months, even though the ultrasound done at the time hadn't indicated any issues. He also said that part of her soft spot was a strange shape, which usually indicates a fluid issue. Hydrocephalus—or excess fluid around the brain—doesn't normally show up until infants are around six to nine months old, which would explain this occurring so suddenly as well. This would also explain her lack of appetite and why she was missing the milestones—because she was in pain. For the moment, it seemed like these explanations were accurate and that a solution was near.

Oh, how I wish he had been right.

9 Bad Series of Fridays

Background Music:
"If You Want Me To," by Ginny Owens

The pathway is broken and the signs are unclear, and I don't know the reason why You brought me here. But just because You love me the way that You do, I'm gonna walk through the valley if you want me to.
—GINNY OWENS, "IF YOU WANT ME TO"

On Friday, January 30, Tori was refusing to eat again, and my motherly instinct was in full gear. I called her pediatrician, and because of the concerns about her head, her pediatrician advised us to go to the emergency room at Penn State Milton S. Hershey Medical Center to push for an MRI. We couldn't wait until May to have one.

I called Brennan and he was able to leave work early; we left as soon as he got home and arrived at the hospital around 3:15 p.m. The nurses and doctors were impressed with how much information I was able to give them and said that many times parents aren't able to recount things. That surprised me because it is my job as Tori's mother to be attentive, and I assumed that all parents would notice changes—especially ones so severe—in their child's health.

Once we got a room, we waited for a bit until two different doctors came in to see her. After hearing her medical history and reviewing what Tori's pediatrician had sent over, they advised a CT scan. She would not have to be sedated for that as she would for an MRI. It took less than five minutes total and she did well. Then we waited. And waited. And waited.

Thankfully we were in our own room and could relax. Teri, my sweet friend from Texas, noticed that I had commented on Facebook about bringing a charger for my phone but not enough snacks, so she had a pizza delivered to us. We were so thankful for the meal, and her kindness eased our stress a little.

When the doctor came in and asked us to sit down, we knew this wasn't just hydrocephalus. She explained that the scan had been read and that while there was no fluid on the brain, there were brain abnormalities. She said that the neurologist would be able to tell us more on Tuesday but that she couldn't really provide any additional insight, as she wasn't qualified to elaborate. In retrospect, I respect the doctor's decision to not speculate, since neurology was not her field of expertise, but at the time it was the most frustrating thing we could have been told. We wanted answers, so not having any wreaked havoc on our hearts. All we could do was wait until Tuesday.

Brain abnormalities—two words that could mean nothing, or two words that could mean everything. Tears started streaming down my face as my mind raced to try to figure out what that could mean. Would she be disabled? Was she going to live? Was it nothing to worry about? Or was it everything?

Brennan and I sat in silence and cried for a long time. Then we prayed and cried some more. We held Tori tightly and watched her sleep. All of a sudden the future we had dreamed of for Tori was slipping away, and we didn't know if we'd be able to stop it.

While we waited to be discharged, my brain wandered and I was reminded of the large percentage of marriages that fall apart in situations like this—I think it's close to seventy-five percent. As I held Tori in my arms, I looked at Brennan and said, "We will NOT let this break us." Right then and there, we recommitted our marriage vows in a way, and we remembered that we are a team. We would get through this somehow, together.

We were sent home with those two words—brain abnormalities—to dwell on for the weekend and tried not to think about what this meant for Tori.

This began a series of very bad Fridays, with the news getting progressively worse as time went on. In the middle of the waiting, I blogged these words:

> Now that we have grieved the unknown future, we are
> trusting the God who knows all . . . the God who loves Tori

and created her and has great plans for her. We are so overwhelmed by the love and support we are receiving from friends around the world. Please pray for Tori. Pray that this is something simple and easily fixed. The thought that our baby might never be the same again is heartbreaking.

Waiting is so difficult, especially when it concerns our precious baby. In a culture that demands instant gratification—something we are now programmed to want and expect—waiting for something so serious is excruciating. And yet we know that we have no control over any of this anyway. God does. God loves Tori more than we could ever love her, and He alone knows her future.

We are finding hope and peace in His promises to us in His Word. He has promised to never leave or forsake us. He has created Tori with His own hand and knows how many hairs are on her beautiful head. He is the Great Physician and is able to heal according to His plan and will. He is sovereign and nothing happens without His consent.

We are also focusing on the positives and not the worst-case scenarios. She is still so alert and her eyes don't miss anything. She is eating well again. She is sleeping better. She was perfect and growing for the first five months.

We realize that this could all be nothing, but we also know that it could be everything. And so we wait and try to stay distracted. We pray and pray. We hold our precious baby girl a little tighter. We thank God for the overwhelming support from our friends and family—and even strangers around the world—during this horrible time. Waiting in the unknown is completely uncomfortable, but we also know that these are the times we grow. And so we wait.

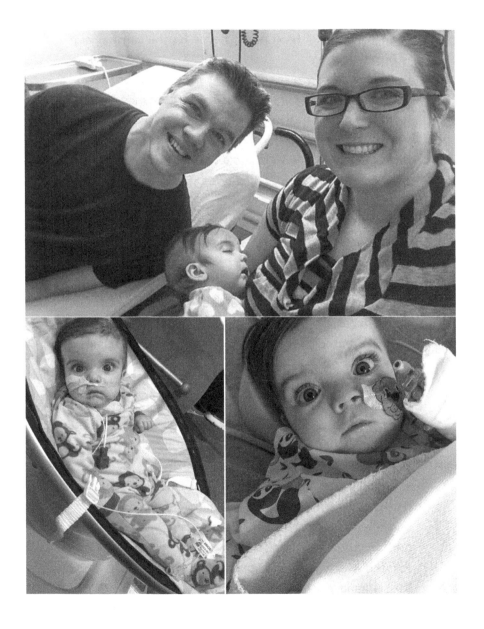

10 The Neurosurgeon and MRI

After we told our parents the news, my mom, DeAnne, decided to fly in from California the next day to help and support us. Having her with us was a great comfort and help because of her servant's heart. She helped us with maintaining the home, running errands, and, of course, caring for Tori.

On Monday morning, we got up early so that we were ready to go if we had any chance of getting her into the neurologist or neurosurgeon before our scheduled appointment. I called the office right at 8:00 a.m. to ask if there had been any cancelations only to find out that they did not have any pediatric neurosurgeons or neurologists in on Mondays; the scheduler said that she would have the physician's assistant look at the CT scan and call me if she could provide insight. She called me an hour or so later and told me that she saw enlarged ventricles, which have produced extra fluid around the brain.

Fluid. The original theory by the pediatrician and the thing the ER doctors said wasn't there.

The physician's assistant said that we would learn more the next day at our appointment but that we shouldn't be too worried at this point because it seemed like it could be easily treated. All at once we felt relieved, angry, worried that they were wrong, annoyed that we had been so freaked out that our baby was going to be permanently affected, and yet hopeful that she was going to be just fine.

Our pediatrician personally called us to get an update and was so relieved to hear what the physician's assistant had said. I had called earlier in the morning to let him know about the "brain abnormalities" comment and he was concerned enough to call us himself.

The following day we met with the neurosurgeon. After evaluating the CT scan, he noted that there was extra fluid in and around the brain and that the ventricles were enlarged. He was puzzled because this wouldn't typically affect development, which made him suspect that something more was happening. He wanted her to have an MRI as quickly as possible.

When we told him that our MRI was scheduled for May 6, he looked at us with amusement and said, "We'll see about that." He worked his magic and got us an appointment for the next morning. The doctor said he would try to read the MRI and get back to us personally by tomorrow evening.

Hope cautiously arose in our hearts once again.

A Mama's Prayer
Blogged on February 3, 2015

Jesus, as I sit and rock this precious baby, I am reminded of all you have done in our lives to bring us to this moment. You brought me to Pennsylvania twice to serve as a "summer missionary" and helped me fall in love with the area . . . You established friendships for me here that would bring me back four years later for two weddings—a trip that renewed my love for the state . . . You put a fire in my soul so that I would move here nine months later . . . You led me to East Shore Baptist Church so that, among other things, I would eventually meet Brennan, nine months later . . . You created us to be perfect for each other, and we got married . . . You allowed us to grow even closer together as we tried and tried to conceive . . . You created beautiful Victoria in your perfect timing and gave her to us as a joyful blessing.

And here we are, a family.

Jesus, we know that you work all things together for your plan and purposes (Romans 8:28). We know that you love us more than we can even begin to imagine. Lord Jesus, our hearts are broken and we are weary. Our precious baby girl is hurting and there are so many unknowns. But we know that YOU know exactly what is wrong. You know the path that we must take in order to bring her back to good health. And we know that you alone know the future you have in store for Tori.

We are trusting you fully with this unknown future because you have proven yourself to be faithful to us time and time again, and we know that you are sovereign. We know that you are good. We know that you love Tori more than we ever could—and we certainly love her SO much.

Lord, let the MRI show exactly what is wrong. Allow it to show the neurosurgeon exactly what he needs to see in order to plan for treatment. Jesus, please create scheduling openings so that she can be treated this week if at all possible. Please help Tori cope with the effects of the anesthesia tomorrow and bring her comfort throughout this process. Ease her pain tomorrow to make it all less scary for her.

Please heal our little girl! Please bring back our happy, developing, playful girl. And most of all, please use this for your glory. We know this isn't happening for nothing—whatever your plan is, we trust it.

Jesus, I am so weary and worn, and most days I feel like I just can't handle this anymore, because watching her suffer is excruciating. I am weak, but I know you are strong. I know that you are there, that you understand, and that is enough. Please, heal Tori.

It may not be the way I would have chosen
When You lead me through a world that's not my home.
But You never said it would be easy;
You only said I'd never go alone.
—GINNY OWENS, "IF YOU WANT ME TO"

The MRI went smoothly and Tori recovered well from the anesthesia. Later that afternoon, the neurosurgeon called to give us the results: he and neurologist Dr. Debra Byler reviewed the MRI and found that the white matter around the ventricles was a slightly different color than it normally is at this age, possibly indicating a metabolic disorder. No pressure from fluid appeared to be there, and there were no masses. Nothing surgical would be required.

He suggested that we meet with Dr. Byler sometime in the next week to start blood tests to determine if treatment is needed. Sometimes these disorders heal themselves, but we wouldn't know until the blood tests were done.

Though I love to research and learn, I refused to Google "metabolic disorder" and decided to wait to see the neurologist to obtain my information. Since we didn't have an exact diagnosis, why worry myself unnecessarily?

We only had to wait two days to see the neurologist, thankfully, and we saw her on Friday, February 6. Dr. Debra Byler earned our respect immediately with her kindness and her obvious expertise. She had already seen the MRI but showed it to us as she explained what was happening. The news we received was devastating: Tori's brain was shrinking and there was a great deal of fluid in the middle of her brain. Dr. Byler informed us that Tori had some form of leukodystrophy, and she added that it was very serious and not always treatable. I knew that *leuko* meant "white," since leukemia is cancer of the white blood cells, but I had no idea what this new word meant.

As the news soaked in, she asked if I wanted to know which leukodystrophy she suspected that Tori had, and I said that I didn't. This was so unlike me, but I didn't want to know until it was a firm diagnosis. I did briefly Google "leukodystrophy" to determine what the word meant and I saw a list of types, but I didn't research further. Additional blood work would have to be done in order to identify the exact type, and that was scheduled for the following week.

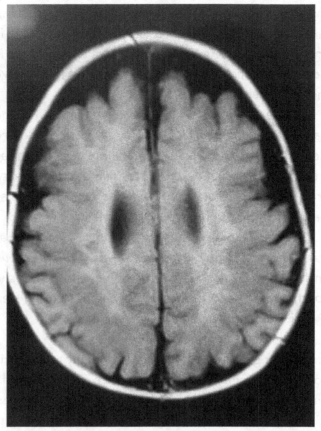

MRI of Tori's Brain on February 4, 2015

We know now, based on paperwork we found, that she knew then that it was Krabbe, but she withheld that information at our request.

As if all of this wasn't hard enough to bear, Dr. Byler asked if we were planning to have more children; when I told her that we were, she gently suggested that we probably shouldn't try to conceive again, because this was likely genetic.

In one moment our world was turned upside down. Not only did our daughter have a serious brain condition, but we were also told that we shouldn't have more children.

In my desperation, I wrote the following on the blog:

We need a complete miracle. We know God is bigger than this! But the thought that we might lose our baby girl is more than we can bear. We are trying to stay strong for her sake, but it is extremely difficult. It can take weeks to get the blood work results back. This is going to be agonizing. To make matters worse, if this is indeed a genetic thing, we may be advised to not have more children.

On the way home, a song came on that had the line "earth has no sorrow that heaven can't cure." We are pleading with God to fix it here and not take her away from us, though that would be the ultimate cure. Please pray for our precious Tori. And please pray for us as we deal with this potentially horrible news.

I can't handle thinking about the possibilities of what might be wrong with our beautiful baby girl. So, I focus on the good things—that she is eating better, that she doesn't need the IV anymore, that she is sleeping well. If I think about anything else, I break down.

Brennan hadn't gone to the appointment with my mom, Tori, and me, because none of us thought that it would be such a devastating day. When I called him to fill him in, he was so upset that his boss compassionately allowed him to go home early. We spent the afternoon trying to remain calm for Tori, because we knew that she was feeling our stress.

Though she had been nursing well most of the week, she refused to eat again that day, and I assumed that it was because I was so upset. I did everything I could to soothe her—and myself—to no avail. After consulting with Tori's pediatrician, it was decided that it was time for a feeding tube (an NG tube, which is inserted through the nose directly into the stomach) to temporarily help her to eat; we were admitted to Hershey Med that evening and assumed we'd only be there for a few hours.

We were there for five days.

Brennan and I continued to just go through the motions, unsure of what to feel or think. There were so many unknowns, so many new things that we had to learn. Thankfully, the nurses who attended to Tori were so gentle and kind; they took care of us, as well, and we appreciated their extra attention during such a tumultuous time.

My dad flew in from California that weekend, and his brother, Patrick, surprised us by driving down from Upstate New York to be with us. Brennan's family came to visit as frequently as they were able.

While we were still in the hospital, we started a public Facebook page that we titled "Tori's Triumph—Team Tori" because of the hundreds of friend requests we were receiving from strangers wanting to follow Tori's progress. My Facebook statuses had been shared by so many people that her story spread around the world without us realizing it. Within a few days, she was being followed by thousands of people!

We weren't sure of many things during those challenging days, but one thing was certain: we were not alone.

11 The Breaking Point

Background Music: "It Is Well," by Bethel, and "Jesus, I Believe," by Big Daddy Weave

When peace, like a river, attendeth my way,
When sorrows like sea billows roll;
Whatever my lot, Thou hast taught me to say,
It is well, it is well with my soul.
—HORATIO SPAFFORD, "IT IS WELL WITH MY SOUL"

As our hospital stay continued to be extended with no end in sight, the stress began to build. With each test they performed, with each specialist who came in to evaluate Tori, the tension inside of me increased a little more. The way the specialists were speaking about Tori was strange, and in retrospect, we can see that they knew that her prognosis was not great.

As we endured all of this, I was so thankful for the presence of our parents, my Uncle Patrick, and my "sister," Cheyenne. Cheyenne came over for a night and spent the following day with me—we even escaped the hospital for a couple of hours—and she helped me get Tori to all of her appointments.

Tori saw an ophthalmologist, Dr. Amanda Ely, who evaluated the anatomy of her eyes. She was so good with Tori and so gentle. There were no indicators of any neurological diseases yet, but Dr. Ely told us that, based on the MRI, she wouldn't be surprised if Tori's vision deteriorated.

She then said, "If she has Krabbe, she will likely go blind." That was the first time we had heard the word Krabbe, and we had no idea what it would come to mean in our lives. I texted Brennan, who was at work, and told him what she had said and added that we should start praying against this Krabbe, whatever it was.

After the ophthalmology appointment, we took Tori to a swallow study they had scheduled for her. It was amusing to me, because they wanted to try to feed her in a high chair so that they could easily view her swallowing using the X-ray machine, but she was not about to let that happen, just as I had told them—she only wanted to be held. The swallow study would determine whether or not Tori was aspirating breast milk into her lungs as she nursed; the results of this study would determine the length of time the NG tube would be her source of nourishment.

We waited a few hours for the results, passing the time with our family and friends. The doctor came in and didn't tell us what we wanted to hear. She confirmed that Tori was aspirating when she swallowed, meaning that small amounts of breast milk were going into her lungs. She also had a limited gag reflex.

This news meant that she would continue to be fed by an NG tube and would likely have to have a tube inserted into her stomach eventually. They did not seem optimistic that this would ever be healed because these muscles are controlled by her cranial nerves, and those were obviously not working.

To say that day was tough is an understatement. In a moment, our entire lives changed for the worst yet again. The baby girl that just weeks prior we had thought was perfect and healthy wasn't perfect anymore. To add insult to injury, I was told that I would never get to breastfeed her again and that she would likely never eat through her mouth. One of the very basic human pleasures is eating, and our Tori would never get to do it.

I remember reaching my breaking point that evening, part of which can be attributed to the fact that I am an introvert and I had been around people constantly for days. Not only that, but I was desperately trying to keep it together for Tori's sake, because I knew that she could tell when I was stressed.

But when the doctor came in to inform us of the swallow study results, that was it. The proverbial last straw. The tears began to flow. I just wanted to be alone with Brennan and Tori as we adjusted to this new normal of feeding tubes and the end of breastfeeding. But the visitors kept lingering and the nurses continued to do their jobs, which felt very intrusive during this vulnerable and heartbreaking time.

Our sweet friend, Laura Furman, had brought us dinner, and her kindness made my tears run freely once more. I could no longer hold them inside. My heart was broken and I so desperately wanted everything to be okay. I simply wanted to be Tori's mom, to raise her, to watch her grow into a God-fearing, gracious, kind, and loving woman.

My parents sensed that we needed to be alone, so they quietly encouraged everyone to leave for the evening. Cheyenne went down to the gift shop and bought us the sign we had admired earlier that read, "Let Your Faith Be Bigger Than Your Fear," and then she headed home.

We cuddled in the bed together, our little family of three, and cried and prayed.

We couldn't imagine how things could get any worse.

> She was fine seven weeks ago. She was normal, happy, healthy, developing. And then January happened. At least we had our baby for Christmas. Then she was taken away from us so quickly. So suddenly. She is still here but just a shell of the girl we once had.
>
> She has even been different since we came to the hospital. Each day she seems to slip further away. She doesn't look at me like she used to. She still wants me to hold her for comfort, but she doesn't look lovingly at me; she doesn't stare into my eyes like she used to. She just "is."
>
> Breastfeeding was taken away from me so suddenly today. And she seems so upset that I am not feeding her. I wonder if that has affected our bonding—does she think I am neglecting her?
>
> I can't even describe my sorrow. I have cried so much tonight and can barely look at her without crying. She is so confused about why I am not feeding her, because she doesn't yet understand the tube. It is so hard and so unfair to her. This is progressing so fast.
>
> And yet, I still believe that God is good. God does

what is best. That He loves Tori and Brennan and me. That He is holding her in His hand.

We are pleading with Him for a miracle. For Him to be glorified through this in such a mighty way. For her to be restored. The Lord gives and takes away, and we are fervently praying that He will give her back to us and take away whatever is destroying her brain.

12 Home Again

Background Music:
"Even If," by MercyMe

After five days of what we referred to as the most expensive vacation we have ever had, we were finally released to go home. While it was a relief because we weren't in a hospital anymore, it was also stressful because we were now on our own with our sick baby.

The home health nurse, Amanda Witmer, spent an hour and a half with us that night, teaching us how to feed Tori at home. Amanda later e-mailed me and told me that she had known that night that the feeding pump was only the beginning of the equipment that would enter our home and that she had been praying for us as we adjusted to this new way of life. She was right, and her wisdom was a blessing.

The feeding tube was incredibly difficult for me to bear. Yes, it allowed her to receive nourishment safely, but it was not fun and it seemed to be so complicated, not to mention that it couldn't feel good for Tori. And, feeding her was MY job, after all, as her mother. I kept reminding myself that we were not the first parents to have to learn how to use a feeding pump and tube, but it still intimidated me.

I was also grieving the sudden loss of breastfeeding, and that surprised me. I didn't realize how much I enjoyed that time with her until it was taken away from me without warning.

We came home to a clean house thanks to my parents and a friend of Brennan's who came over to clean our house that day. We had meals in our fridge and freezer for much of the upcoming month, thanks to our church and our family and friends. One of our friends, Kristin Piarulli, had set up a meal list for the following two months, as well. We were astonished by the generosity of those who gave money to help us pay any bills that came in. Our home was filled with flowers and cards to brighten the atmosphere. All of these things served to lessen the stress of our new normal, and we were so grateful.

I wrote these words in an attempt to describe how we were feeling:

> No parent wants to watch their child suffer, and if she has what they suspect, great suffering—and a short lifespan—may occur. But in all this, we are choosing each day to trust God completely. We may have our moments, like Tuesday night as we wept, where we ask questions and grieve: however, throughout our lives we have seen God at work in such mighty ways, and we KNOW that He is in control. I constantly have to remind myself of that right now, and I am so thankful for the promises of His Word. He has a plan that is great and He has chosen us to be part of that story. We are so thankful to be Tori's parents, even if things aren't going like we had hoped and dreamed. She is a gift, and we pray that God will heal her and bring back her smile, vision, laughter, personality, and health.

All along we had decided to be completely transparent as we blogged about each test result and each piece of bad news that we received. Brennan wisely noted that we couldn't help anyone else if we were being fake. I wanted to be real in my writing and not appear to be a faith-filled supermom who isn't emotionally affected by the deterioration of her baby.

As we waited for the blood work to come back, I blogged about how Brennan and I were coping:

> I have cried more in the past two weeks than I have in the last twenty years combined. Denial is the easiest place to be right now. Ignoring the MRI results, ignoring the fact that our baby's brain is not functioning properly. Ignoring her feeding tube (while still caring for her, of

course). It's just how we're dealing with all of this for the moment.

The thought that our beautiful, happy, smart, talkative, smiling baby may never be returned to us is beyond devastating. When I see the videos of her from a couple of months ago, it brings tears to my eyes because I miss her SO much. Being a stay-at-home mom to Tori has been the best thing that I have ever done. She has brought me so much joy and I can't believe how much I love this little human. Obviously, I still love her and that will never change. But I miss her. I miss her personality. I miss watching her learn new things. I miss her smile and her squeal when she was excited. The thought that she might never be like that again is more than I can bear. I know Brennan feels the same way.

The thought that she might never recover is unfathomable.

We are pleading with God to do a miracle—to completely heal her brain and give her the best possible quality of life. If she ends up being a person with special needs, we will rejoice in the fact that we at least get to keep her here on earth with us.

For now, I am living minute by minute and cherishing my time with her. We are celebrating the little things—like her improvement in terms of eating with the feeding tube and other little things. Thinking past today becomes overwhelming because we have no idea what we are facing.

We are certain that God has a purpose for all of this, and we know that He loves her more than we ever could.

We were told about a clinic in Milan, Italy, that is the only place in the world currently treating kids with certain types of leukodystrophy using stem cells. If that ends up being her issue, you better believe that she and

I are headed there. They have apparently successfully treated thirteen children thus far. We are also SO encouraged about how we have been connected with several specialists and experts already just through people sharing Tori's story on Facebook. And Team Tori day was incredible! Seeing all of the photos with the sign was such an encouragement because we were reminded that she is being prayer for by thousands of people.

Yes, we are in more pain than we have ever experienced before, but we also are constantly reminded—and remind ourselves—that our God IS greater than this. He created the whole world and has raised people from the dead. He can easily heal Tori if it is His will.

Oh Lord, we continue to plead with you for a miracle, for a complete restoration of our beloved daughter's brain and body. You have set the stage perfectly for something magnificent to happen and for thousands of lives to be impacted through the healing of our Tori. Her doctors would be astounded to see her suddenly able to eat normally, to talk and smile again, and to develop as a six-month-old should, given her potential diagnosis and the hopelessness that comes along with it.

Lord, we prayed for her to be given to us for years. You were faithful and gave her to us last July, and we have cherished each day with her and will continue to do so. Lord, please repair her brain and restore her! Please heal our Tori and use her to change the world before she can even talk!

We continued to remind ourselves of God's faithfulness and love to compete against the voices telling us that things weren't going to be okay. It was a mental battle like none other, one that took months to overcome. Why is it that we fight the hardest against the things we cannot change, even when we know that God is ultimately in control?

13 Diagnosis Day: The Day Our Lives Changed Forever . . . Again

Background Music:
"Tell Your Heart to Beat Again," by Danny Gokey

Waiting has never been my strongest skill. When I was younger and anticipating a trip or church camp or the first day of school, sleep often eluded me and my mind would race in excitement as I pondered what was about to take place. Adrenaline would be my fuel the following day to compensate for the lack of rest.

We had been told to expect the blood work results to take two or three weeks to come back, and it was explained that the lab liked to be entirely sure of the diagnosis before releasing the information to the parents, which we understood. While we wanted to know immediately what was happening to our daughter, at the same time we didn't want to know. We didn't mind this waiting. Waiting made it feel like the inevitable was further away. We were in a holding pattern that was acceptable to us at the time. Two weeks of blissful ignorance sounded great.

So when we received a phone call less than twenty-four hours later, on Friday, February 13, we knew this was either really good or really bad news, and we had a feeling we knew which type it was.

The nurse asked if we wanted to wait until February 24 for our scheduled appointment to receive the results or if we wanted to come in immediately. That was an obvious decision and we made an appointment for a couple of hours later.

When the neurologist came in to talk to us, we knew it was bad. You could see it in her eyes. She was dressed in plain clothes, not her typical white doctor's coat. She wasn't supposed to be at work that day. She was somber and unsmiling. All of this was a recipe for disaster.

Dr. Byler shook our hands and then said the most terrible words we could have heard:

"It's Krabbe."

Krabbe is a form of leukodystrophy, meaning the white matter of the brain shrinks due to defective genes. In the case of Krabbe, the body doesn't produce an important enzyme called galactocerebrosidase—or GALC—which protects the myelin, which in turn protects the entire nervous system.

We had heard about that disease from the ophthalmologist earlier that week, who said, "If it's Krabbe, the vision usually goes."

We had briefly Googled *leukodystrophy* after the previous neurology appointment and remembered seeing Krabbe on the list.

We knew that word meant certain death.

My mind was racing, and I kept telling myself, "There must be something we can do. Something. Anything."

I will never forget looking over at Brennan, who was holding Tori tightly, as those words were spoken. He was broken. The pain in his eyes was tangible as he asked the question we both wanted to ask but neither wanted the answer to: "How long does she have?"

Dr. Byler was kind and gentle and said she couldn't say for sure and that there are many forms of Krabbe. Further genetic testing would be required. She explained the genetics of Krabbe—that both parents have to carry the defective gene in order for a child to have the disease. She said many other things that day that went right over our heads, because when you've just been told your child is going to die, you can't really pay attention to much else.

Dr. Byler then gently restated that we might want to reconsider conceiving again, given the odds of Krabbe appearing in any of our future children (25 percent chance per pregnancy, according to genetics). That was a lot to process in one day.

We were devastated beyond words. Hopeless. Knowing Tori was given such a grim outlook left us numb. The doctor gave us a few minutes by ourselves and we wept together, clinging to our bright-eyed, beautiful, precious daughter whom we now knew was dying.

Dying is not a word that should describe anyone's six-month-old child.

I remember being in utter disbelief that my world was being shattered into a million pieces. I remember pleading with the Lord to save our daughter, the one for whom we had prayed for so long. Desperation is the perfect word to describe how I felt. I didn't want to lose Tori, and I was willing to do anything to keep her here. But there was nothing that could be done. We live in a world where there's almost always something that can be done to fix a problem, right? Not this time.

I was desperate to wake up from a nightmare that had only just begun.

When we went home, we cried and cried. I sat in the glider for what seemed like hours, holding and rocking Tori so tightly, never wanting to let her go, tears streaming uncontrollably down my face. I gave up on trying to be strong for her, which we had tried to be because we knew that babies can sense stress and other emotions in their parents. I couldn't do it anymore, even for her. In a way it felt as though I were grieving not only for myself, but for Tori as well, because she surely knew that something had changed, that she couldn't do things anymore, that she had an uncomfortable feeding tube in her nose. But she was unable to express anything except pain now, so I cried on her behalf.

It was the beginning of an unexpected and unwanted journey, and we were afraid. Numb. Devastated. Grieving. That was to be expected. We were living in a nightmare that we couldn't escape. Our baby was dying and there was nothing we could do. Nothing. There was so much we didn't know then, so many fears that existed in our hearts and minds. And now I faced the prospect of not only losing my baby, but of never being a mother again.

The weeks leading up to diagnosis day were gentle in pace, and each week prepared us a little more for what was inevitably coming our way. Each Friday we heard increasingly bad news as the diagnosis was narrowed— first, brain abnormalities, then leukodystrophy, then Krabbe. In hindsight, these steps made the final blow of a terminal diagnosis a little easier to bear than if it had come out of nowhere. Each diagnosis was another perforation in our hearts, preparing us to be broken more gently instead of completely shattered all at once.

We told our parents and siblings the news and then I blogged about the results. That post traveled around the world, literally, and was viewed by over thirty thousand people that day alone. Tori's story was resonating with people, and her eyes drew them in.

Word travels quickly within the leukodystrophy community, and some of Tori's followers had already been following other Krabbe children or were parents of Krabbe children themselves. One of those parents, Tammy Wilson, wrote to me and immediately offered her support. She added Brennan and me to a Facebook group solely for Krabbe families—a group that became our lifeline at times—and the other families welcomed us in with open arms, saying, "I'm sorry you have to be here, but it's a great place to be." We had become part of an exclusive club, one filled with reluctant members who would do anything to have never been included.

That evening, as Tammy was messaging me, she asked if I had contacted Dr. Maria Escolar yet, and I told her that we didn't even know who she was. Tammy explained that she was one of the leading experts in Krabbe and that her practice was in Pittsburgh—only three hours from us. She gave me her phone number and strongly urged me to contact her. Now. By this time, it was 9:30 p.m. on a Friday night. I was exhausted and still reeling from the news only hours before, so I asked Tammy if she would pass our information along to Dr. Escolar so she could call at her convenience.

Dr. Escolar called us thirty minutes later, around 10:00 p.m. on a Friday night.

She listened to my recap of Tori's medical history leading up to the diagnosis and said that she wanted to see her right away. If we'd bring Tori to her, they would run tests and do another MRI to determine if Tori was transplant eligible. Hope was restored with that thought—that perhaps Tori's Krabbe was treatable after all!

She began to set everything into motion and asked us to wait to hear from her nurse practitioner on Monday before making any official plans. I told Brennan and my parents about the call, and we knew we had to go to Pittsburgh. We had to try. After being told that there was nothing we could do to fix it, being told that there was a slight chance meant everything.

For the first time in weeks, waiting wasn't excruciating. For now, waiting felt like hope.

14 What Is Krabbe Leukodystrophy?

Let's take a brief moment to talk about what Krabbe is before we proceed. I have often joked that I should receive an honorary nursing degree for everything I have had to learn since Tori became sick. Hopefully this chapter will answer your questions and make the chapters that follow a little more clear.

As I mentioned briefly before, Krabbe is a form of leukodystrophy—*leuko* meaning white, and *dystrophy* meaning abnormality. It is also called globoid cell leukodystrophy. Essentially, the white matter of the brain shrinks due to defective genes that cannot produce the necessary levels of an enzyme.

Krabbe is a recessive gene, and both parents must carry the gene in order to pass it along to their children. Genetics will tell you that the chances per pregnancy of two carriers having a baby with Krabbe are one in four, but the leukodystrophy experts believe it is much higher. More often than not, they see repeats in families, which is why we were advised to not have more children. There are a few options available to us to ensure that any future children do not have Krabbe, but none are ideal and most are exceedingly expensive.

Why is it that those who want to be parents the most are often the ones who cannot be?

There are over one hundred gene mutations that cause Krabbe, and Brennan and I carry the exact same one—the 30-kb deletion. We were told that the odds of winning the lottery are better than the odds of us meeting and getting married with the same exact gene mutation.

We are fortunate in the United States to have two experts right here. People travel from all over the world to see Dr. Escolar at Children's Hospital of Pittsburgh of UPMC (University of Pittsburgh Medical Center) and Dr. Kurtzberg at Duke University in North Carolina.

There are several forms of Krabbe, the most common being early infantile, which presents around five to six months of age or earlier. Early infantile Krabbe is also the most severe, causing death around or before the age of two. This is the form that Tori had.

As the disease progresses, the brain becomes unable to perform simple bodily functions such as muscle movement, vision, swallowing, breathing, temperature regulation, and hearing. The babies also endure nerve pain throughout their bodies, which is why they are very irritable. It can also cause seizures.

Krabbe damages the myelin in the brain and once it gets to a certain point, it is irreversible. The damage has been done. There is no cure.

There is, however, a life-saving treatment. The only catch is that it must be caught very early, preferably at birth before the disease has been able to do a great deal of damage.

If a baby is diagnosed with Krabbe and is transplant eligible, a stem-cell transplant can be performed through the bone marrow and the body will begin to produce the GALC enzyme. Doing the stem-cell transplant can stop the progression of the disease but cannot reverse any damage already done.

I know what you're thinking: If there's a treatment, is Krabbe part of the newborn screening tests that are done in the United States?

Currently, only six states screen for Krabbe: New York, Missouri, Kentucky, Tennessee, Ohio, and Illinois. Pennsylvania will only screen for it at the mother's request. Several other states have passed legislation but are not yet enforcing it.

Why aren't states screening? Some argue that the testing isn't good enough yet because it can't immediately differentiate between being a carrier and being affected and further genetic testing is required. One state argued that the follow-up testing would cause undue stress on the parents as they awaited the results. Undue stress? I'm sorry, but undue stress is finding out that it's too late to try to save your child's life when they could have treated it at birth!

Others argue that the treatment isn't good enough even though it has a high success rate. We counter with this: by not screening for it at birth, and by not providing transplants for as many babies as possible, how are you going to improve treatment? Is it risky? Of course. But when the alternative is death, what do you have to lose? By not testing, they are robbing parents of the ability to TRY to save the life of their child, leaving them instead feeling hopeless and devastated.

Lives are at risk every single day because diseases like this are "rare" and states don't want to spend the money on the tests. On average, it costs less than $6 per child to test for Krabbe and other treatable leukodystrophies. I don't know a single parent who wouldn't pay $6 to be certain that their child was healthy.

All right, let's dive back in where we left off.

15 The Days After

Background Music:
"Lord, I Need You," by Matt Maher

The day after diagnosis, I was barely functioning. It was all I could do to care for Tori and continue to learn our new routines with medical equipment and feeding tubes. I was comforted by the songs playing on the radio, as each one spoke to our situation so well.

We had so many unannounced—but well-intentioned—guests that day, and that was so very difficult for me because I felt like I had to be "on" constantly. I had to field questions. I had to be kind and gracious when really I just wanted to hold my baby by myself and cry.

I remember being in a daze. Being an introvert and hearing news like this can be challenging because people care and therefore want to be physically present to comfort you, but that's not what is best for you at all. It's likely what *they* need to begin to understand this horrible new reality, but it isn't what you need.

Despite the grief we were working through, both Brennan and I remarked that we felt at peace. Of course, this doesn't mean that we immediately accepted Tori's fate and didn't struggle against it, and it certainly doesn't mean we didn't cry. It became a constant mental battle, one that can still rage today—a battle between what we know to be true, that God is good and loving, and what we feel, which is deep loss. Yet, we felt a peace we truly couldn't explain—the peace that God's Word promises, a peace that surpasses all that we can understand when we trust in Him:

> *Always be full of joy in the Lord. I say it again—rejoice! Let everyone see that you are considerate in all you do. Remember, the Lord is coming soon. Don't worry about anything; instead, pray about everything. Tell God what you need, and thank him for all He has done. Then you will experience God's peace, which exceeds anything we can understand. His peace will guard your hearts and minds as you live in Christ Jesus. (Philippians 4:4–7)*

We began receiving messages about how Tori was already impacting the lives of people we've never even met, which reminded us that God was already using her little life for big things.

All of these things combined with the hope that we felt gave us strength in the midst of weakness and pain. We knew that He was going to heal her—whether on earth with us or in heaven with Him. It didn't make it easier, but it brought us comfort, and we put our trust in the loving, good God that we know and serve.

Portrait Session by Katie Bingaman Photography

♡

We continued to receive visits from well-meaning friends and family as the days went on. Thankfully, those who visited didn't linger; they were loving, generous, and thoughtful, and we were so amazed at their kindness to us.

And that was just the beginning—we learned through this journey that, in hopeless situations like these, some people feel the need to do something tangible, something to feel like they are making a difference when nothing else can be done. We have seen so much good, so much kindness, so much compassion as we have walked through this diagnosis.

A few days before Tori's diagnosis, we began receiving gift cards and donations. I had posted a status of gratitude during our hospital stay because Penn State Hershey Medical Center has a Starbucks and I was in desperate need of caffeine. After that post, we received over $200 in Starbucks gift cards in less than twenty-four hours! I wasn't sure what to do, because I knew that once I got home, I wouldn't be able to get coffee very often and we had been given so much already.

As my Uncle Patrick and I walked down to the Starbucks inside the hospital, I mentioned to him that I wasn't sure if we should post something and say that "we're good" in terms of gift cards or not, and he gave me some wise advice that would impact our lives for the next fourteen months (and beyond).

He said that we should never tell people to stop giving, because giving helps them feel like they are being helpful in a helpless situation. Giving is their way of loving us and supporting us in the smallest of ways, and telling them to stop would rob them of the blessing and joy of giving.

I pondered his words and realized that he was right. I had felt that we were being greedy by not asking them to stop (since we had been given plenty), but greed was not present. There is a fine line between being greedy and being a gracious receiver: greed thinks about what it is getting out of the situation, whereas being a gracious receiver means that you are more focused on the giver and the joy they receive by giving to you.

We had no idea just how many opportunities we would have to receive graciously over the next fourteen months, especially. People we knew and many we didn't blessed us with meals, gift cards for gas and restaurants (and coffee), clothing and giraffes for Tori, house cleanings, and so much more, including thousands of dollars to a GoFundMe account that was set up for us as a surprise. It was overwhelming and humbling to see how much people cared about our family. The kindness of others truly got me through the first two weeks postdiagnosis and beyond.

One of the greatest gifts we received was a unique one: breast milk. The stress of Tori's diagnosis (as well as the fact that she hadn't been nursing well) dried up my milk supply, and I was having difficulty pumping enough milk for her daily needs. They had tried formula in the hospital, but her belly didn't adjust to it well. Brennan had mentioned this to his coworker, Emily, who has a daughter around Tori's age and she told him to follow her home after work because she had breast milk in the freezer!

If you have ever breastfed a baby or attempted to pump, you know what a gift this was. We posted a note of gratitude about it on Tori's page and messages poured in from moms all over the country who also wanted to help feed Tori! My dear friend, Alli Muller, sent thousands of ounces from herself and her friends throughout Tori's life! We were amazed at how God continued to care for us in these seemingly small but truly amazing ways.

Breast milk was gentle on her stomach and great for her immune system. Thank you to every mom who has ever donated breast milk to feed another baby—it's an amazing gesture!

God was caring for us, just like He promised.

16 Headed to Pittsburgh

Background Music:
"Make a Way," by I Am They

On the Monday following diagnosis, we confirmed our plans to head to the Children's Hospital of Pittsburgh to have Tori evaluated by Dr. Escolar and her team. Brennan was unable to get off work for the week, so my parents accompanied Tori and me. We boarded the train on the Tuesday with hopeful hearts and weary souls.

We chose to take the train because it was winter and snowstorms were in the forecast, and because of Tori's strong dislike of the car seat. It worked out really well and she slept the entire time, likely due to the gentle rocking motion of the train and being held constantly.

Before we left, someone who was following our story contacted us and asked if there was anything they could do to help us out while we were in Pittsburgh, as they were locals. This woman—Molly Howard—offered baby equipment, meals, whatever we needed. I mentioned that we would need a car seat while we were there, and she went above and beyond to make it happen. She didn't just leave it at our hotel: she found out from the hospital which car company would be picking us up from the train station, asked them to come pick up a car seat (and installed it!), and sent a care package from her family for our use during the trip. During subsequent trips, this same family was such a blessing to us. Her husband drove us to and from the train station, they brought us meals, and they sent notes of encouragement all along the way. Once strangers, but now family through the love of Christ. This brought such joy to our hearts.

After a short night's sleep, we left the hotel in single-digit weather and traveled to the hospital. When we entered the waiting room of Dr. Escolar's clinic there was another family there, the Schroeders. I watched them feed their son, Blaine, who was in a special stroller and had a feeding tube. I watched their demeanor, their calm spirits, and reminded myself that I could handle whatever was to come, including the dreaded feeding tube.

That morning began a series of tests, including another MRI, to assess the progression of the disease and the extent of the damage. Tori wasn't allowed to eat most of the day because of her MRI at 2:00 p.m., so I had a cranky baby who didn't understand why she wasn't being fed. The physical therapist and speech therapist started their evaluations and poor Tori was tired, hungry, and didn't want to be put down (as usual), so it made it difficult for the team to assess her.

At that point, Dr. Escolar came in and we got to meet her. As I watched her interact with Tori and her team, I felt calmer. This woman cares deeply about these Krabbe children and so desperately wants to find a cure (and she's close!). She decided that it would be a good idea to start Tori on a medicine to help her muscles relax. Most Krabbe babies end up on two medicines (at least)—gabapentin for nerve pain and baclofen for muscle tone—and Tori was already on the first one. She said that we could possibly see a totally different baby emerge after the baclofen was in her system, and that we might even see her smile again. Hope.

The physical therapist and Dr. Escolar looked at Tori's body and tested range of motion and other things. She then gave me a head-to-toe report of what she noticed. Dr. Escolar and her staff were kind and patient as they explained everything to us, sometimes multiple times, and helped us get a better grasp on what Tori was going through. I think they understand well the mental state that parents are in when they first come to see Dr. Escolar, as it is often immediately following diagnosis, and they don't mind answering questions repeatedly.

Tori had her MRI after their evaluations. Once she was awake, they let us go back to see her and she was surrounded by nurses talking about how beautiful she was. She was very calm and just lay there for quite a while, wide-eyed and alert.

The next morning started with a meeting with Dr. Escolar, where she went over the MRI findings as well as the genetics behind this disease. She is a wonderful teacher and definitely an expert. Then she told us what she saw on the MRI and the spinal tap: Tori was beginning stage three (of four) of early infantile onset Krabbe, and stage four would begin in months, not years.

Prognosis: death by thirteen months of age.

As if that wasn't difficult enough to hear, she then gently explained that Tori was not a stem-cell transplant candidate because of how advanced the disease already was. Dr. Escolar said that the process of the transplant (chemo, etc.) would accelerate the disease for Tori. From that point on, our focus would have to shift from hoping for a transplant to simply trying to make her as comfortable as possible while the disease took its toll.

I gazed into Tori's big, beautiful eyes and I was filled with emotion, unable to imagine not looking into them for the rest of my life. When she was born, I wanted what any parent would want: to watch her grow and learn, to make friends and learn about Jesus, to experience the simple and extravagant joys of life, to travel the world with us and explore.

Now I simply wanted her to live.

Even when I don't see, I still believe.
—Jeremy Camp, "I Still Believe"

We headed back to Harrisburg feeling disappointed but also more confident in caring for Tori and easing her discomfort. The NG tube was becoming more familiar (especially after two ER visits while we were there due to the tube being clogged and then inserted incorrectly by the nurse), and my parents were a great help with the rigid schedule she was on for feedings and medications. My mom stayed with us for five weeks total, and my dad stayed for three. They cooked, cleaned, maintained the home, and helped us adjust to our new normal. What a gift.

As each day passed, and as I surrendered this situation to the Lord, my burden became lighter and lighter. I continued to feel His peace and love surrounding our family, and I made a daily decision to continue to trust Him with all of this. And it really was a decision, something I had to force myself to do because it was certainly not what came to me naturally in the beginning of this journey.

I have been a follower of Jesus for most of my life. I have attended church since I was born and officially became a Christian when I was eight. Throughout these years of walking with God, I have seen Him do amazing things. I have seen Him keep His promises time and time again and watched as He worked all things together for good (Romans 8:28). I have watched His plans for me unfold and have always been amazed at how things turned out, because there were many times when I could not see what He was doing. I could only see the trees when He could see the forest.

I could list example after example of His work in my life; Brennan could do the same.

And now we were journeying along an undesirable path. We pleaded with God daily to change the course. Losing our daughter is absolutely not what we ever saw coming, and our hearts were broken over the prospect of being childless again.

We knew (and know) that God had placed parenthood in our hearts, and we were so happy to finally welcome Tori into our family. We never expected this.

> *His timing is not our own, and it is perfect.*
>
> *His thoughts are not our thoughts, and His ways are not our ways (Isaiah 55:8–9).*

Trust is built over time in any relationship. God has never failed us and we know without a doubt that He loves us. We trusted God and His plan, but that didn't mean that we weren't struggling with any of this. On one hand, we continued to hear how Tori's life was impacting people and how God was already changing thousands of lives through her. We praised Him for that and were humbled that He would use our family in that way.

But we also asked why it had to be her. Why us? Why did we have to lose our daughter for these lives to be impacted? Why didn't He heal her and change the world through her testimony? What an amazing display of His power that would have been! But we don't know what His plans are, and sometimes that's for our protection. During those weeks immediately after diagnosis, the trees were looming overhead, and our perspective was limited—there was no way to see the entire forest.

I reflected on our situation on our blog:

> We have never loved anyone like we love this tiny, precious human. We cannot imagine our lives without her. Yet we know that God loves her, and us, and that He has an amazing plan for her. And we are choosing hope over despair, because we know that God is sovereign and we trust His plan.
>
> And so we wait. We pray. We trust. We love her and each other. We cherish each moment because we don't know how many moments remain. And we are thankful for whatever time we are given with our precious Tori.

17 Medical Decisions and a Mama's Heart

Background Music:
"Worn," by Tenth Avenue North

It didn't take long for us to be forced to make some difficult decisions about how to best care for Tori. We had to decide whether or not to put her through a surgery to insert a G tube for her feeds as well as have a Nissen wrap (where part of the stomach is wrapped around the esophagus to prevent anything from refluxing) done to prevent her from throwing up (which Krabbe babies do often, and they can aspirate what they throw up). We ultimately agreed to both procedures, but it was a difficult decision because her life expectancy was so short. We also were assigned to the palliative care team at Penn State Hershey Medical Center, which is known as the Hummingbird Program.

Essentially, the Hummingbird Program is for children who have chronic or terminal illnesses. They provide support to the entire family as well as the child. We discussed comfort care for Tori and pain management. We were given a prescription for morphine and Valium to use if she was in terrible pain that the other meds weren't relieving.

In that moment, I was forced to reenter the reality that our daughter was dying. There was a fine line between living in hope for a miracle and living in the reality that our baby girl had a terminal illness . . . that her life expectancy could likely be counted in months, not years.

The pain we experienced was palpable at times.

We began discussing what to do if God chose to take her home—a discussion we didn't finish at first because it was too difficult. No parents should ever have to plan their baby's funeral.

As I recounted the day on our blog, I wrote this and prayed with every fiber of my being that it would be our reality: *"Some of the best Bible moments are the impossible situations that are followed by the words, 'but God . . .' We are praying that this is one of those times."*

On February 27, I wrote this prayer:

> Thank you, Jesus, for the beautiful gift you have given us in Victoria. Lord, I want to watch her learn to crawl, walk, and talk. I want to watch her learn to enjoy food and how to cook. I want to see her learn how to ride a bike, learn to read, learn everything. I want to nurture her innate talents and gifts and help her discover her passions. I want to teach her to love music, to teach her to sing and play instruments, and to worship through music. I want her abilities to surpass my own.
>
> I want to see her grow up and become a beautiful young woman. She is so beautiful now—I want to watch her become gorgeous both inside and out. I want her to become a teenager and all that comes with that. Attitudes, independence, makeup, sleepovers, boys that Brennan will chase away. After all, she isn't allowed to date until she's thirty. I want her to see what an amazing, godly, wonderful man her father is and to choose a husband just like him.
>
> I want her to graduate from high school and pursue her dreams—whatever those may be. I want to teach her to love to travel and explore. To love other cultures and learn from them. To use a camera to capture images that have impact.
>
> Most importantly, I want to see her use her miraculous healing as a powerful testimony to bring the kingdom of God to those who do not yet know you. I want to see her grow in wisdom and grace as she follows you, Lord.
>
> Oh Lord, we continue to plead with you for a miracle,

for a complete restoration of our beloved daughter's brain and body. You have set the stage perfectly for something magnificent to happen and for thousands of lives to be impacted through the healing of our Tori. Her (many) doctors would be astounded to see her suddenly able to eat normally, to talk and smile again, and to develop as a seven-month-old should.

Please heal her, Lord Jesus. Allow her to experience all this life has to offer. Allow her to testify of your mighty power for many decades here on earth. Please, Lord, allow us to not just be parents, but to be HER parents. To raise her and love her for the rest of our lives. We know that you alone can restore life to her brain and heal her body, and we ask you for this miracle. In Jesus's name . . .

We adjusted to our new normal and continued to fervently pray that God would heal our Victoria, here on earth and not by taking her to heaven so soon. I prayed both silently and through writing on the blog:

We have found as parents that you develop sayings and nicknames in your family without really planning to do so. They just come naturally and become part of your family's language and culture. One of the things I have found myself saying to Tori in recent months is, "I love you . . . Do you know that?" Rationally, I know that she does to some extent. She trusts me. She calms when I hold her. I am her mother and I know that she is bonded to me in a unique way. She must feel loved in some innate way—at least I pray that she does.

But my heart longs to hear or see a response. Some acknowledgment that she feels my love, that she feels safe, that she is content. That she isn't scared or lonely. That she knows we love her deeply. I'd happily take a teenage eye-roll with an exasperated "yes, Mom" if that meant she could communicate to me. But she can't show us anymore. That ability was sadly taken from her . . . No longer can her eyes light up and a smile cross her face when I walk into the room; no longer can she laugh and show her joy.

Instead, she is now trapped inside her deteriorating body, unable to exhibit any emotion except pain (which is exceedingly rare, thankfully). Have I mentioned that I hate Krabbe? She still communicates in her own ways and we have had to learn her new, limited language. But it's just not the same—for her or for us.

More than ever before, I find myself longing for heaven (as is mentioned many times in the Bible—this world is not our home and heaven will be so amazing). I think about what it will be like in heaven and what it will be like to reunite with her should she not be healed here on earth. When I think about seeing her there, I often picture a scene where we run to each other and embrace. She looks so much like me when I was younger and has pigtails in her hair. Her eyes are still big and beautiful like they were before Krabbe—eyes like a Disney princess.

When we step back from our hug, she smiles and simply says, "I know you love me, Mama. You always have." And in that moment I feel peace.

18 Patience, Grace, and a New Kind of Love

Background Music:
"Your Hands and Feet," by Justin Gambino

I have been learning a lot about grace in the past few years—mostly pertaining to how infrequently I offer it in my daily life. The book *Grace* by Max Lucado was eye-opening; I was so challenged by it when I read it a few years ago (it really is a must-read). A practical example? Most of my early driving years were in Southern California. If you've been there, I don't have to say more. I am much less aggressive after living in Pennsylvania for many years.

I have found that patience and grace go hand in hand: for example, being willing to be patient with people is often a form of grace (think Bill Engvall's "Here's Your Sign" stories). I always try to remember that I often don't know the backstory behind someone's behavior or attitude, and that helps me to be graceful toward them . . . usually. Do they deserve my patience and kindness? Yes.

When I became a parent, I was amazed at how naturally patient with Tori I became (I now believe that God gives mothers an extra dose of patience and grace for their babies, especially given the sleep deprivation that accompanies motherhood). Granted, she was also the perfect baby for the first four months and was rarely fussy or irritable. She didn't sleep much, but she was at least happy about it.

Throughout the first few months of Tori's increased/constant irritability and decreased sleeping hours, I had to make a conscious decision many times a day to show a new level of patience and grace toward her and the situation. She couldn't help how she felt and she didn't have any other way of telling me that she was uncomfortable.

I fully admit that the first two weeks of this behavior change were frustrating and I was not very patient. I initially assumed that the fussiness was simply a growth spurt, teething, or something like that, and given that I hadn't had a full night of sleep in about ten months, its constant presence wore me down quickly.

However, it is amazing how the word *terminal* can totally transform your attitude in an instant.

I began to recognize that a day might come when I would do anything to hear that cry again. To be up all night with her, as sleep deprived as I would be. To comfort her and hold her. Just one more time.

I prayed that this lesson wouldn't fade away as quickly as it came, because it applied not just to Tori, but to everyone I met. We have no idea how many days are left in our lives or the lives of others. We cannot imagine what impact our kindness and patience may have on someone's hurting heart.

And so, grace continued to be the primary lesson the Lord was having me learn during the wonderful journey of motherhood with Tori. Motherhood is often accompanied by lessons of selflessness, humility, and patience. And I am so thankful for the changed person I became, even though the lessons weren't easy.

Brennan and I went through what felt like a lifetime of emotions in the first three months of this unwanted journey. From such joy and love in seeing our baby grow and learn to sorrow and grief over her terminal diagnosis. We realized that we were living out our wedding vows in a completely new way—"in sickness and in health, till death do us part." I never thought about that phrase applying to how we love our children as well.

It is so easy to love a happy, healthy, growing, developing baby. My heart would overflow with joy when she would smile and laugh and babble. It was effortless.

I quickly found that loving a terminally ill baby girl is completely different. It looks different and feels different. It almost has to be different.

My love became protective, fierce, strong, desperate, deliberate, focused on helping her manage her pain rather than helping her learn new things. I knew that I had to choose to show love and grace even when she didn't let me sleep, when she wouldn't stop crying, and when I couldn't put her down.

In my exhaustion and desperation, in my moments of grief and sorrow, I had to choose to love her and put any feelings of frustration at the situation aside. I learned that so much of what we think "can't be helped" is actually a choice we can make. I had to remember that she was the one in pain, the one whose brain was deteriorating, the one who was losing her sight and other functions.

And in those moments, I would cry out to God and pray for two things: first, that He would completely heal her and show the world His power through her little life; second, that if He would choose to take her home with Him, that she wouldn't suffer and that He would do it sooner rather than later for her sake.

Brennan and I forced ourselves to talk about the "what ifs" and the possibility of needing to plan a funeral. Of needing to decide upon a burial (but where?), cremation (a thought I couldn't handle), donating her body to science if it would be beneficial for Krabbe research, or an alternative (did you know that you can have ashes made into diamonds?). We hated talking about these things, but we also didn't want to have to make these types of decisions after her death.

These discussions forced us to learn more about heaven, and the more we learned—through the Bible and through the book *Heaven* by Randy Alcorn—the more we agreed that, even though we desperately wanted to keep her here, we knew without a doubt that heaven was the best place for her—and any of us! No pain. No sorrow. No sin. No hardship. She would be able to hang out with Jesus and would be there to meet us whenever it was our time to go. Our separation would only be temporary!

God gave us such a peace about that possible outcome, as undesirable as it obviously was. He reassured us that, no matter what, He wanted what was best for Victoria. While we couldn't see how that outcome would bring good to our lives, we could at least see the good in it for her.

And so we continued on this undesired journey, taking it one day at a time, trusting the Lord even when we didn't understand and didn't like what was happening. Our faith became so much stronger and it would continue to grow. We continued to love her and to love each other, and, most of all, we held on to the hope of a complete healing for our baby girl.

Marriage experts will tell you that it is vitally important to maintain your marriage during the child-raising years because one day it will be just the two of you again. One day you will need to know how to live with each other and love each other without your children around.

After Tori's diagnosis, Brennan and I began learning day by day how to maintain our marriage in light of the fact that it might be the two of us once again sooner than we ever imagined. Are we perfect? Nope. We fail daily. But it is through those failures that we have learned many lessons, and we have grown stronger and closer together.

We share these things in hopes that they will encourage someone else who is walking a similar path. Many of them we learned by observing other couples, and we are so thankful for their wisdom. Of course these are all things couples should do under normal circumstances, but when you are subjected to a tragedy or other stressful season, it is even MORE important to be purposeful about maintaining your marriage.

So, how are we caring for our marriage?

1. We established from the beginning that this would NOT break our marriage.

The evening of January 30, 2015, as we sat in the ER awaiting results from Tori's CT scan, I looked at Brennan and whispered, "We won't let this break us." He readily agreed. We made a decision before she was even diagnosed to not let the enemy use this to break us apart. It was like a vow renewal in a few simple words.

We made the daily choice to walk through this together, because we promised to do so from the beginning. For better or for worse, for richer or for poorer, in sickness and in health. We believe these vows don't only apply to the two of us: *they apply to our children as well.*

We had our first child together and we were losing her together. *Together.*

You don't make marriage vows because it's a romantic thing to do; you make them because life is hard, times can get tough, and the promise you made is a constant reminder that you are in this together.

2. We communicate openly, honestly, and freely throughout this journey.

Because we are different people, this has affected Brennan and I differently, so it has been very important to be real always. If we are having an emotional moment, we talk about it. If we are struggling with some aspect of our situation, we talk about it. If we can't figure out why we are feeling a certain way, we talk about it. There's no reason to hide our emotions considering all that we've dealt with, yet we know that is a temptation for many couples. It's easier to just put our feelings aside and ignore them.

Every day since diagnosis we had to face the reality that our daughter was dying, and it wasn't something we could ignore. We acknowledged the situation even then, and we worked through the process of grief together as much as we could.

3. We try to apologize quickly when our emotions speak for us.

When you are losing a child, the grief begins at the moment of diagnosis. At least it did for us. We have found that there are often underlying emotions that shape our tone of voice and our words without us realizing it at first. Therefore, we do our best to analyze our feelings to find the root cause, because often it is our grief that caused the outburst of emotion, not what the other person said or did.

4. We forgive each other freely and offer abundant grace.

Grace is probably the most important element of any relationship, but especially for situations like ours. Offer it freely. Remember that you are both dealing with the most traumatic situation you have ever dealt with, and it is new territory.

5. We were creative with our time to ensure that we still "dated" even though we couldn't leave the house.

Because we never had in-home nursing care, we didn't get many date nights. We didn't even sleep in the same bed, because if we did, we would both be exhausted all the time since Tori seemed to hate sleeping. Because she had to be close to one of us always, she slept on one half of the bed and one of us slept on the other half. The other person slept upstairs in a guest room so that they could get some rest. This was our reality, and we made the most of it.

So, in order to still "date" each other, we found a show to watch weekly and laughed together as we enjoyed it. We also regularly took advantage of Tori's typical evening nap, ate dinner together, and did whatever we could to spend quality time together.

It isn't about quantity in this season—it's about the *quality*.

6. We allowed the primary caretaker to have some alone time whenever possible—and we took care of the caregiver.

I cared for Tori about eighteen hours every day by myself, and I needed opportunities to get out of the house. Running errands—which I previously didn't care to do—became such a joy for me because I was able to do things by myself, things that otherwise got neglected.

I would drive when we went anywhere as a family; Brennan would sit in the back to care for Tori. These seemingly small things allowed me some time away from being a caretaker while still doing things that were productive and beneficial for our family. As an introvert, this alone time recharged me and allowed me to be the best possible caretaker and mother for Tori that I could be.

Brennan also did his best to do things to take care of me, as we realized that I wasn't feeling cared for—by no fault of his own! Because my entire life was spent caring for Tori and for him, it was important to have him do little unexpected things to care for me as well—things like making chiropractor appointments for me. These little things helped ensure that I was taken care of in the midst of our crazy life.

As we walk along on this undesired path, we will continue to learn more about ourselves, our marriage, and how to make it even stronger. We will continue to share those lessons along the way, because we want to help others as much as we can through their own tough situations.

Every day we do our utmost to choose joy and love instead of allowing sadness and irritation to prevail. We make every effort to be a team instead of individuals. We remember and honor the vows we made before God, family, and friends. And we find reasons to be thankful even when it would be easier to complain.

Our marriage is not only going to survive this tragedy, but it is going to thrive because of our purposeful care of our relationship in the middle of all of this. And yours can, too.

19 Healing in Different Ways

Background Music:
"Even If (the Healing Doesn't Come)," by Kutless

Fridays hadn't been kind to us in the first two months of 2015. We were told that Tori had brain abnormalities on a Friday. Tori was given a nonspecific leukodystrophy diagnosis on a Friday. Tori was admitted to the hospital on that same Friday. Tori received her Krabbe diagnosis on the following Friday. We were told that Tori was already in stage three of Krabbe the Friday after that. We had a lot of bad Fridays in early 2015.

In March, however, Fridays were redeemed for us. Brennan had the day off and we were able to spend the day together thanks to two wonderful friends who not only came to our home to watch Tori but did some cleaning as well. We have been blessed beyond measure by our friends and family, and this was a huge example of that.

We went to the chiropractor for much-needed adjustments and then decided to have lunch at the Chocolate Avenue Grill in Hershey. We enjoyed our conversation and we managed to speak about things other than Tori for once. That is difficult enough for parents of healthy children, and it was especially difficult for us. When it came time to pay our bill, the waitress came over and told us that another table (whose occupants had already left) had paid our bill. We owed nothing. We assumed that this was a random act of kindness and were so blessed by this gesture.

When we opened up the folder to see the receipt, however, there was a note inside. We were both in shock, not only because this has never happened to us, but because the women at that table clearly knew who Tori was. Who we were. It wasn't that we had shared our story with them over lunch or anything like that. They must have been following Team Tori on Facebook and recognized us from there.

Both of us were trying not to cry at that moment. To this day, we do not know who it was, but their generosity and kindness—and prayers, as the note indicated—meant so much to our hurting hearts.

That same evening a fund-raiser was held in Tori's honor, raising over $3,500! It was organized by Brennan's coworker and friend, Jessica Kline, and many others. There were hundreds of people in attendance, including another Krabbe family in our area. Our hearts were so encouraged and we were yet again reminded that we were not alone.

Nothing is impossible for You; You hold my world in Your hands.
—KARI JOBE, "HEALER"

Our culture has become increasingly obsessed with instant gratification and three-step formulas to solve any problem. With the technology available to us today, we are able to find answers to just about anything in a matter of seconds. Or, we can find a formula that will lead to answers or success if only we "follow these three steps."

I don't know if it's a result of the American Dream and the ideas ingrained in us as Americans from birth, but we have certainly come to expect in the American church that we are entitled to an easy life. We become frustrated when God doesn't solve all of our problems, when He doesn't answer our pleas for miracles. After all, we deserve it!

We have become so conditioned to get what we want when we want it—waiting is nearly unheard of in our culture today. Waiting is a discipline that so many of us lack. Just look at the amount of consumer debt in our country! People are impatient.

I know this mentality has leaked into my prayer life and into my expectations of God, as hard as I try to fight it. As I prayed about Tori and her healing, my thoughts often wandered to wondering if there were steps I was not following, as if there were magic words that would instantly make everything better. Obviously, that is not biblical and I know that. But it happens.

There are very few things I haven't been able to accomplish or obtain in life with a little hard work and perseverance. This is not to say that things have always gone my way, but I have rarely been in situations so out of my control that there was nothing I could do to change the outcome—until this.

I had never felt so powerless in my entire life. No amount of money could fix her damaged brain. No amount of love could restore her to perfect health. No amount of hard work and effort could make a difference in her nervous system. Nothing . . . except God.

As I pleaded with the Lord to spare Tori, as I tried to bargain with Him (I'm human, after all) and convince Him that He should allow her to be healed here on earth, it occurred to me more than once that this situation was so unbelievably out of my control. There was literally nothing that I could do to change the outcome.

As I read the dozens of messages that came in from people about dreams they had about Tori's earthly healing, I realized how much I wanted to see my own prayers do something big like this, in person.

So often we pray for others passionately and see God move from afar. But I wanted to see Him move up close—in my daughter's life.

The Bible tells us that faith in Him can do amazing things:

> *Then Jesus told them, "I tell you the truth, if you have faith and don't doubt, you can do things like this and much more. You can even say to this mountain, 'May you be lifted up and thrown into the sea,' and it will happen. You can pray for anything, and if you have faith, you will receive it." (Matthew 21:21–22)*
>
> *The apostles said to the Lord, "Show us how to increase our faith." The Lord answered, "If you had faith even as small as a mustard seed, you could say to this mulberry tree, 'May you be uprooted and be planted in the sea,' and it would obey you!" (Luke 17:5–6)*

We knew we were facing impossible odds from an earthly perspective, but we know and believe that with God ALL things are possible! Krabbe was our mountain. Krabbe was our mulberry tree.

I watched Tori regress and I observed her pain, and my mind desperately sought the secret code, the perfect combination of words that God was waiting to hear. And I wanted Him to heal her NOW, not later. I wanted Him to conform to my wishes, my desires, my timing.

But our God isn't like that.

Our God created time and He doesn't operate within our concept of it. The Bible tells us this:

> *But you must not forget this one thing, dear friends: A day is like a thousand years to the Lord, and a thousand years is like a day. (2 Peter 3:8)*
>
> *For you, a thousand years are as a passing day, as brief as a few night hours. (Psalm 90:4)*

In anything we face during this life, we must trust the timing of the One who created time. The same God who created everything we see is the same One who holds us in His hand, and He knows our future. He isn't a God of formulas or magic spells.

When Jesus healed in the Bible, it was because the sick believed in Him and that He could do it. They had faith. Jesus didn't heal everyone instantly in the Bible—there were a few situations where He waited so that His power could be displayed in greater ways: Lazarus. Jairus's daughter. His own resurrection. The wait was always worth it. We know that His timing and methods are perfect, no matter how hard the waiting may be.

Waiting requires humility. Humility is essential, as is a healthy understanding of God and His will and purposes for us. We don't deserve anything. Paul's thorn never went away, as far as we know. If God allowed Paul, one of the greatest missionaries, to have an imperfect life and didn't answer his every prayer favorably, then why should we expect to have a different outcome?

If I am honest, I will admit that I am very skeptical of God giving the gift of healing to people in the world today. I absolutely believe that He, Himself, can heal and often does. But because I have seen so many phony healers in my lifetime, I am doubtful about a person having that gift.

Yet, when your child is dying, you will do anything to save his or her life. Tori's diagnosis made us consider things that we previously would have pushed aside, and we opened our hearts to the possibility of the gift of healing being present today in hopes that God was trying to show us His power in a new way.

We heard from many of Tori's followers about this church where healings reportedly happened consistently—a church called Bethel in Redding, California. I was amused by this because Redding is only thirty minutes north of my hometown of Red Bluff, California. We were told about people who had come from all over the world to be prayed for at Bethel and we would only have to drive thirty minutes.

Since we were already planning a trip to California in April 2015, we decided to make a trip to Bethel. What could it hurt? When we went to Bethel, Tori was nine months old. From a medical perspective, she had fifteen months or less to live. Fifteen months. Or less. And yet, we knew—and know—that God is greater than Krabbe.

We felt hopeful. Maybe this was God's plan, especially since so many unrelated people had suggested that we go to the same place. Brennan and I knew that Tori's healing would be such an incredible testimony of God's power to tens of thousands of people around the world, especially to the doctors who have been working with us. Can you imagine what an impact it would have had for them to see a new MRI of her brain and have it be completely restored? And to see her developing and growing normally again? We felt hope for the first time in weeks.

Our hope increased as we had what seemed to be a divine appointment on our flight from San Francisco to Redding.

We sat in the front row of the plane on that flight, and there was a woman across the aisle from us, by herself. During the flight, the flight attendant saw us feeding Tori through the tube and asked us questions about our situation.

The woman across from us was listening, and when we got to the baggage claim, she approached us. She said she had heard us telling Tori's story and that she was on staff at Bethel. She asked if we had heard about their healing ministry and we said that we had and that we were planning to go. She exchanged contact info with us and asked us to text her when we arrived so that she could bring us right in. She said she would arrange a special prayer team for us because of the life-and-death nature of our situation. She also prayed over Tori right there.

So my mom, Brennan, Tori, and I went to Bethel that Saturday and she kept her word.

I can't remember her name but I can still see her face. While we waited for the prayer team to arrive, she told us that she was originally supposed to be farther back in the plane but that she had felt God tell her to move to the front. To be by us. Hope.

The team prayed over Tori for complete restoration and healing, for victory over Krabbe. They then prayed over Brennan and me for healing of our DNA so that we might be able to have more healthy children. It was an interesting and peaceful morning, and we left there feeling hopeful, praying that none of this was coincidence but rather God's orchestration.

Soon after this, I was reading John 11:1–44, the account of Jesus raising Lazarus from the dead. I was encouraged by this passage and specifically by these things:

- God would be glorified through Tori's life, whether He healed her here or not. He is always working and we know that—we just hoped His plan was to keep her from impending earthly death.
- Even if His plan wasn't to heal her here on earth, we knew she would be with Jesus forever and that we will see her again someday. Like Jesus said of Lazarus, ultimately her sickness will not end in death—eternal death, that is.
- Even in her grief, Mary and Martha demonstrated faith in God's power. I had always read their statements as being accusatory— trying to make Jesus feel guilty for not being there; now, however, I think they were simply acknowledging their faith in who He was—God.

Even as they mourned their dear brother, they still knew the truth about who Jesus was and they clung to it. They were mostly right in what they said: "Lord, if only you had been here, my brother would not have died. . ." (John 11:21); the difference is that Jesus could have healed Lazarus from anywhere, not just by being there (as in Luke 8 with the centurion's servant).

And that is what gave us hope: absolute faith that God could heal Tori from anywhere. It didn't have to be through one specific person or any special prayer. If it was His will, He would do so, whether through the medical community or through humanly unexplainable healing.

I wrote this on April 23, 2015, a few days after going to Bethel:

> "What do you mean, 'If I can?'" Jesus asked. "Anything is possible if a person believes." The father instantly cried out, "I do believe, but help me overcome my unbelief!" (Mark 9:23-24)
>
> I wonder if the father in this passage felt the same way that I so often do—so desperately wanting his child to be made whole again, knowing that Jesus can do it, but afraid to be hopeful.
>
> Afraid.
>
> More often than not, my prayer is that of the father in this account: I believe, but help me overcome my unbelief! I waver between knowing without a doubt that God can heal her here on earth and yet doubting that He will.
>
> I have discovered that I am afraid to be hopeful, despite our experiences in the past few days and with how God seems to be working. I am still trying to pinpoint the cause of the fear, but I think it comes down to a fear of being disappointed in the outcome, a fear of being disappointed in God—whom I love and trust implicitly—if He takes her home to heaven instead of allowing us to keep her, even though I do trust His plan and do not doubt that His plan is best for all of us. I think fear is to blame.
>
> Fear is easy; hope is excruciating.

What we are going through is completely unnatural. Parents aren't supposed to lose their children. As someone who doesn't even know how it feels to lose a grandparent yet (yes, I am blessed to still have all four!), the thought of losing my only child is incomprehensible.

I wonder if my fear of being hopeful is a defense mechanism. I am afraid to hope that God will choose to heal Tori here on earth, despite the fact that every fiber of my being desperately wants that to be the outcome.

Hope is hard. Hope is vulnerable. It seems irrational in a situation like this.

Fear is comfortable, expected, the rational response.

And yet, I remind myself that we serve the same God who healed/heals the sick and who raised people from the dead! Jesus Himself was resurrected after being in the tomb for three days! Nothing is impossible with God. Nothing!

Jesus repeatedly told His disciples to not be afraid, and that nothing is impossible for God. That is what I force myself to remember daily—it isn't impossible for Tori to be healed!

The struggle continues, and I pray that I can overcome the fear of being hopeful, because I know that God is love, He is good, and His plan is best. I don't know if Jesus meant belief in Him or absolute belief that healing would happen; but I do know that He loves Brennan, Tori, and me. And whatever He has planned will be okay in the end.

As we walked through this season of knowing that we were likely going to lose Tori, it was tempting at times to be frustrated with God. We were truly never angry with Him, but there were times when it seemed like He was so far away, like He was ignoring our prayers. Sometimes it felt like we were alone.

The unanswered prayers for Tori to be healed weren't the ones that caused the frustration: it was the simple prayers, like the ones for her to sleep so that we could sleep, because our continual sleep deprivation began to wear on us. It seemed like something so easy for God to do, and yet He didn't answer them the way we wanted Him to answer.

As Christians, we are constantly asking God to make things easier for us—and while there's nothing wrong with asking for those things, sometimes we lose sight of the fact that we're constantly asking for Him to do things instead of asking how we can serve/learn/grow through these things.

Who are we to ask God to change His mind? We have no idea what He has in store (read Isaiah 40 and Job for great insight into this). We can't even imagine how He is going to use Tori's life (and our lives) to impact the world! If He took this cup from us, would His impact on the world through her/us be the same?

When we think about it like this, it almost feels selfish to have prayed for God to heal her (almost—it's obviously not selfish to want to keep your precious child).

We pray that God will continue to use this situation to impact the world, to grow His Kingdom though Tori's precious life, that there will be VICTORY through Victoria even if there wasn't an earthly healing victory FOR her.

Your will be done . . .

20 *Routines*

Background Music:
"Every Good Thing," by The Afters

We had a wonderful visit with my family in California, and Tori was able to experience the Red Bluff Round-Up (the world's largest three day rodeo) festivities, including the Kiwanis Club Pancake Breakfast, which is a family tradition. She cuddled with her uncle Kenny, my brother, and of course, my parents. She also got her first haircut, thanks to her great-aunt Sandee. My mom's sisters—Karen, Donna, and Lori—all came to spend time with her, and she also got to visit with all of my grandparents—Ken and Pat Close and Fay and Ruth Eskridge. It was an amazing, love-filled trip and we were so thankful.

When we returned from California, we were finally able to settle back into daily routines and a schedule that made our lives easier, even though it was rigid.

The frequency of appointments outside our home greatly diminished, allowing for a much more relaxed lifestyle. Early Intervention came to our home weekly to provide physical therapy, occupational therapy, nutrition consults and weigh-ins, and vision therapy. I loved that we, the parents, were in charge of what therapies Tori had. We had the right to say no (though we never did), and we had plenty of freedom. They were there to help Tori and to help us help Tori.

During the first intake appointment, the coordinator, Rose, told me that there was another Krabbe family nearby, but she obviously couldn't be specific. She said they lived very close to us and I was amazed because it's considered to be a rare disease. I gave her full permission to pass our information onto this family so that we could connect.

I heard from the other family very quickly, and they lived less than two miles from us. Tori was the second baby (that we knew of) in our township to be diagnosed with Krabbe, and that is remarkable, given the supposedly rare likelihood of inheriting the disease.

I looked forward to these Early Intervention visits as friendships developed between the therapists and me. The visits were truly highlights in my week. They all loved Tori and enjoyed helping her. Diane, Cheryl, Kelly, Erica, and Colleen made my weeks much more interesting and fun. Not only did these therapies improve Tori's quality of life in many ways, but they also allowed her to express her personality in unique ways.

Of all of her therapies, vision quickly became my favorite to observe simply because of Tori's obvious enjoyment of it and the reactions it elicited. Most of the time she would pay attention and look at whatever Cheryl was showing her that day. However, if she didn't approve of the new item, she would close her eyes and pretend to be asleep! At first we thought she was truly asleep, but after a while we caught on. She would peek out to see if the item she didn't like was still there, and if it was, she would close her eyes again. If we had taken it away, she would keep her eyes open. We found so much joy in her attitude! Cheryl was incredibly creative and found ways to utilize everyday things—or things from the Dollar Tree—to entertain Tori. Tori's visual understanding actually IMPROVED over the course of this therapy, and Dr. Escolar was so surprised.

Similarly, we learned that Tori would communicate with us about the things that she loved. It started with a stuffed giraffe that lit up—when the light would go out (after five minutes), she would start whimpering. If I didn't respond, the whimpering would turn into an all-out cry. After I'd turn it back on, she would stop crying and look at the giraffe, wide-eyed. That giraffe—now named Victor—became a staple in our home, and we obtained duplicates just in case we ever lost one! As a side note, it is because of Victor being in nearly every picture we posted of Tori that she became associated with giraffes. Whenever people saw them, they thought of her and often purchased giraffe-related items to send to us.

The vision therapist helped us better understand cortical visual impairment and how we could help stimulate Tori despite the fact that her brain wasn't processing images well. Tori loved light, so she gave us many creative ideas to try.

The goal of physical therapy was to find solutions to make life more comfortable for Tori. Diane offered creative—and effective—solutions for bath time, sleeping, and relaxing. We learned ways to work on putting her down more often, techniques for stretching out and massaging her hands, and teaching her to rest her head on both sides instead of just her right side. We discovered that it helped if we gently got her attention before touching her or trying to pick her up, to prevent her from startling or becoming upset.

Diane also helped us obtain important pieces of equipment, like Tori's adaptive stroller and stander, and her letters to our insurance company were convincing enough that they paid for everything in full! We were astounded because we had heard story after story from other Krabbe families about insurance battles. The Lord certainly blessed us with our insurance provider, because they never turned anything down for Tori.

Kelly, the occupational therapist, used two innovative therapies on Tori to help keep her swallowing muscles firm and to move her sacro-spinal fluid around to help alleviate the pressure in her skull.

Most of these women shared our faith in Jesus, and that made the visits even more precious because I was able to be so open with them about the work we saw God doing.

After some time, the feeding tube became routine and easy, just as the experienced Krabbe families had said it would be. We never regretted our decision to place a G tube in her stomach or to have the Nissen procedure done. We would still allow Tori to taste things whenever possible—things like Cheetos, Dum Dum lollipops, and the fried apples from Cracker Barrel were her favorites.

Tori was stable and her disease didn't seem to be progressing as quickly as expected. At Tori's three-month follow-up in May, Dr. Escolar admitted that she was surprised at how well Tori was doing and even said she was doing better than she would have expected. Once again, hope flooded our hearts as we so desperately hoped that God was healing our baby girl.

Unfortunately, a devastating progression of the disease was about to reveal itself, and we were completely unprepared.

21 The Suction Machine

Bad things always seem to happen at the worst possible times. And for us, they seemed to prefer Fridays as their day of choice.

Tori began to lose her ability to swallow on June 5, 2015. Not only was it a Friday, but it happened around 4:00 p.m. I had been able to go days without thinking about the reality that Tori was dying. She had been so stable, so calm, so content. Our days were falling into a routine, and things were as good as they could be.

We knew it would come sooner or later, but it was a rude awakening when she started to have difficulty swallowing that day. The suck-and-swallow reflex is a "use it or lose it" ability, which is why we almost always had her sucking on a pacifier. We were advised by the Speech Language Pathologist at Hershey Medical Center in February (prediagnosis but post–swallow study) to do so in order to help her maintain those abilities as long as possible.

Four months later, she still had both abilities, but her swallow reflex began to fade rapidly and without warning. We had already started the process of obtaining a "suction machine" for her to help her get rid of saliva and phlegm when she could not swallow it. This machine prevented her from aspirating anything, which is crucial because aspiration can lead to pneumonia, and pneumonia would likely lead to death.

However, we didn't have the machine in our home the day that Tori began to struggle to swallow, and because it was a Friday afternoon, we couldn't get a delivery until Monday morning. Throughout the weekend, we once again felt helpless. All we could do was listen to her carefully and do our best to help her get rid of excess saliva with the nasal aspirator bulb.

Yet again we were reminded that she was fragile, that she was dying.

It reminded me to continue to pray diligently and without ceasing for Tori, because in the busyness of caring for her, it was easy to forget to do anything else, including prayer. Full days went by in which I forgot to say even a short prayer for her because I was so focused on her needs; I had forgotten that the greatest thing I could do was pray to the only One who could heal her.

The suction machine would become an increasingly important part of our lives, and as much as we hated that we even needed to use it, we were so thankful for its existence.

22 Motherhood and a Treasured Moment

Background Music:
"Thy Will," by Hillary Scott and the Scott Family

Intense love does not measure, it just gives.
—Mother Teresa

I always knew that motherhood would be a selfless endeavor. From the very beginning, your body, your time, your thoughts—everything revolves around, and belongs to, your children.

Before I became a mother, I had an idea about what it looked like to be selfless and I knew I could handle it with the Lord's help. After all, a mother's love is one of the strongest forces on earth, and I was ready for the challenges.

I had no idea just how "selfless" my life would become when Tori became sick.

By the way, I don't write this to invite pity or sympathy, or even accolades. Rather, I have continually strived to be transparent during this journey in hopes that someone will be encouraged or challenged by how the Lord is speaking to our hearts and working in our lives.

Here is a glimpse into what daily life with Tori looked like most days:

6:30 a.m.: feed Tori (forty minutes)
8:00 a.m.: give first med
9:00 a.m.: give second med
9:30 a.m.: try to shower quickly
10:30 a.m.: feed Tori
11:30 a.m.–2:30 p.m.: Early Intervention (not daily)

2:30 p.m.: feed Tori and give first med
3:30 p.m.: give second med
4:30 p.m.: maybe start dinner
5:30 p.m.: Brennan gets home
6:30 p.m.: feed Tori
7:30 p.m.: bath time (every other day)
8:30 p.m.: family time (maybe)
9:30 p.m.: give first med
10:30 p.m.: give second med and feed Tori
11:30 p.m.: hopefully sleeping

In between all of these things, I was also doing the following:
giving eye drops
putting face cream on
putting splints on periodically
suctioning Tori's mouth
cleaning spit-up
changing diapers
changing her position
turning her giraffe back on all the time
doing vision and physical therapy
holding her for hours if she needed or wanted to be held
updating Team Tori while she slept in my arms
putting essential oils on her feet and diffusing them
maybe getting one chore done
maybe eating meals
preparing her milk for the next day
venting her G tube when she heaved

And the list goes on . . .

I rarely slept. Brennan and I took turns sleeping (and didn't sleep in the same bed for fourteen months), so on nonwork nights for Brennan, I would get to sleep upstairs (one to two nights per week). To say that I was exhausted is an understatement. Before the onset of Krabbe, the normal newborn-stage sleep deprivation was bearable because Tori was such a joy, such a delight. I didn't mind nursing her every two to three hours, because she was always so happy, so content. Watching her learn and grow filled my heart with enough energy to endure the sleepless nights (and days). Her smile and laughter would bring my heart a palpable joy and my heart would overflow with love. But once Krabbe took full force, I felt drained constantly.

When Tori was healthy, I was still able to do things for myself (like shower and eat a good lunch) because she was content to play with her toys on her own and would nap without being held for twenty to thirty minutes at a time. I could still take care of our home and do things for myself like shop, read, eat meals, and so forth.

My view of what selflessness means changed drastically in January 2015.

> *"For even the Son of Man [Jesus] came not to be served but to serve others and to give his life as a ransom for many."*
> —MARK 10:45

My days became a blur, much like the lives of those with healthy babies, but there was no tangible "reward" for my selfless service anymore. My days revolved around medication and feeding schedules, appointments with specialists and Early Intervention therapists, and keeping Tori comfortable, which usually entailed rocking her in our recliner most of the day. If I was lucky (or if someone came over to hold Tori), I could take a five-minute shower while Tori stared at her light-up giraffe on her pillow.

Eating didn't always happen—at least not healthy eating. I rarely left the house, because Tori didn't like being in the car and it became increasingly difficult with all of her equipment, so I didn't go grocery shopping unless I went at night when Brennan was home, which meant sacrificing time with him. Thankfully, I discovered that our local grocery store would deliver groceries for a nominal fee, so that service became an incredible blessing to our family. Still, the stress, the sleep-deprivation, lack of exercise, and poor eating habits caused me to gain unwanted weight, and there was little I could do differently.

Doing simple things for myself didn't happen at all. As much as I wanted to work on Tori's Project Life albums (an alternative to scrapbooking for less creative people such as myself), read my Bible (as in the paper version, not on my phone), or even CLEAN MY HOUSE (yes, I actually longed to do normal things like that), they couldn't happen until Brennan was home for the evening, if at all. And even then, I struggled between wanting to clean my house / do things for myself and wanting to spend time as a family doing other things.

I didn't stop to think about how little I was doing for myself very often, but when I did, I became overwhelmed by the energy my life required. I went from such an easygoing, low-maintenance life (even with a baby) to a life that was so high maintenance that it was overwhelming at times.

I don't like this, I don't want this, and I keep praying it's all a nightmare. Yet I don't think about how hard it is as I am living it—I just do it. Though my priorities have shifted drastically in the past three months, I know that I have to find a balance because I need to take care of myself while also caring for Tori.

Through all of this, I am continually learning to praise the Lord in the midst of these difficult and unwanted circumstances because I know that He is using them to refine me and to make me more like Jesus. Does this mean I like what is happening? No. Does this mean that I am a perfect Christian mother and entirely unselfish? Ha. Definitely not. But I trust that He is redeeming this terrible situation in ways we can't even imagine. I trust that I will be a more loving and selfless person because of all that we are going through. It's a moment-by-moment process of surrendering my own desires for what is best for Tori. It isn't easy, I'm not perfect at it, but thankfully we serve a God who showed us what selflessness looks like when He sent His son, Jesus, to our world two thousand years ago, and that same God is just as full of love, grace, and mercy today as He was then.

Is there any encouragement from belonging to

Christ? Any comfort from his love? Any fellowship together in the Spirit? Are your hearts tender and compassionate? Then make me truly happy by agreeing wholeheartedly with each other, loving one another, and working together with one mind and purpose.

Don't be selfish; don't try to impress others. Be humble, thinking of others as better than yourselves. Don't look out only for your own interests, but take an interest in others, too.

You must have the same attitude that Christ Jesus had.

Though he was God, he did not think of equality with God as something to cling to.

Instead, he gave up his divine privileges; he took the humble position of a slave and was born as a human being.

When he appeared in human form, he humbled himself in obedience to God and died a criminal's death on a cross.

Therefore, God elevated him to the place of highest honor and gave him the name above all other names, that at the name of Jesus every knee should bow, in heaven and on earth and under the earth, and every tongue declare that Jesus Christ is Lord, to the glory of God the Father.
PHILIPPIANS 2:1–11

I began to live my life with my "hands empty, eyes up," and I would only focus on doing "the next thing" instead of being overwhelmed by the entire list, as my friend Amy Smoker taught me. The concept originated with Elisabeth Elliot, who gleaned this wisdom from an old Saxon poem:

Do it immediately;
Do it with prayer;
Do it reliantly,
casting all care;
Do it with reverence,

Tracing His Hand,
Who placed it before thee with
Earnest command.
Stayed on Omnipotence,
Safe 'neath His wing,
Leave all resultings,
DO THE NEXT THING.

It was easy to be overwhelmed by the enormity of our situation and I had to consciously make small decisions and take small actions. I would do one thing at a time, then I'd do the next thing. I surrendered my exhaustion and my fear to the Lord and He sustained me. I have no idea how I got through it all, and that is a huge testament to God's constant presence in our lives.

I chose to live moment by moment, day by day, and I did whatever I could to serve my daughter as selflessly as I could, knowing that she was suffering more than I could begin to imagine, and knowing that Jesus Himself lived a completely selfless life to redeem us and be our perfect example. It truly was the least that I could do.

When Tori was healthy, there was no doubt that she loved me. She would smile and talk to me, and her eyes would light up when she saw me—I knew that was her way of telling me how she felt. After Krabbe came into our lives, the only way I could tell that she loved me was this: she would immediately calm down when I picked her up. Even the Early Intervention ladies took note of that and were impressed. But I missed the smiles and coos, the laughter.

One night, as she was calming down after being startled (a frequent occurrence), she put her hand on my arm. It was a small thing under normal circumstances, but it brought tears to my eyes. I had Brennan come take a picture of the moment so that I could always remember it.

It could have been a complete coincidence, but I am choosing to believe that it was intentional.

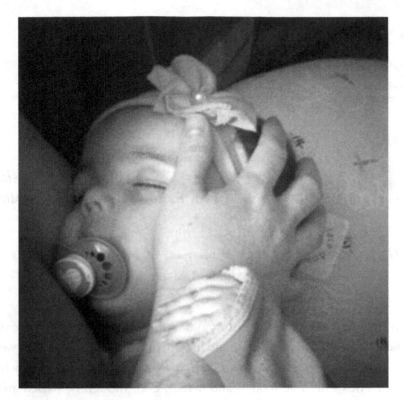

It is so hard on this mama's heart to watch my baby be in pain and to see her fading away. She is a mere shell of who she used to be, and I miss her personality so very much. To not see her expressions of love anymore has broken my heart over and over.

Unless God intervenes, I will never hear her say "Mama" or see her smile again. I will never get to hear her say she loves me. I try not to dwell on those thoughts, but they creep in from time to time.

I know she trusts me and needs me even though she can't show me in the same ways anymore. I know that.

What I am learning is that she is trying to show me—I just have to learn her language.

23 Plans Far Greater . . .

Background Music:
"I Will Follow," by Chris Tomlin

He works things together for His purpose and not our expectations.
—HEATHER ZEMPEL, *AMAZED AND CONFUSED*

Both Brennan and I love the history of Hershey, Pennsylvania, and of the founders, Mr. Milton S. Hershey and his wife, Catherine. To me, they were truly two of the greatest humans who have ever lived. Milton Hershey has become one of my role models and heroes, even though he passed away thirty-seven years before I was born. More than any other figure in history, I wish that I could sit down with this man and just listen to him speak. He only had a fourth-grade education, and yet he built a great town that all works together for the well-being of children in need. His vision and his compassion were remarkable, and he was well before his time with his ideas and his values.

Milton chose Derry Township, Pennsylvania, as the location for his factory because of the rich farmland and the abundance of dairy farms. He soon realized that in order to attract workers, he'd need to provide them with a place to live. So he created Hershey as we know it today. He built homes, parks, services such as banks, a laundry, churches, a transportation system, and so forth, so that his workers would have a great life living in Hershey.

Milton and Catherine were unable to have children of their own. They believed that wealth was meant to be shared and to be used for the benefit of others, and when they realized that they had far too much money on their hands for their liking, his wife suggested that they start a school and make that their family. And so they did.

In 1909, they started the Hershey Industrial School and took in orphaned boys to educate them and teach them skills (such as farming) to ensure that they would succeed in life.

Milton continued to grow the chocolate company to ensure that the school would be funded. He also began organizing his other ventures into what is now known as Hershey Entertainment & Resorts to secure additional funding sources, and he separated the chocolate company (now known as the Hershey Company) from the entertainment division to protect the school.

Most amazingly, he and his wife loved these children so much that they gave their entire fortune TWICE (totaling around nine billion dollars) to ensure that the school would exist in perpetuity.

Today, the Milton Hershey School largely operates off of the interest from this endowment, in addition to the profits from the Hershey Company and Hershey Entertainment and Resorts, and the endowment is invested by the Hershey Trust.

One of my favorite quotes from Mr. Hershey is this: "If we had helped a hundred children, it would have all been worthwhile."

During Mr. Hershey's lifetime, he saw enrollment at the school increase to one thousand! Today, the school is home to over two thousand students. There are over 180 student homes (each housing nine to twelve students), each run by a houseparent couple to ensure that the students feel like they are part of a family as opposed to being in a dorm-type environment. In 2016, the ten thousandth graduate walked across the stage at graduation. What a legacy.

> *Well, I have no heirs—that is, no children, so I decided*
> *to make the orphan boys of the U.S. my heirs.*
> —Mr. Hershey

When you buy Hershey's chocolate products, visit Hersheypark or the Hershey Gardens, stay at The Hotel Hershey or the Hershey Lodge, or golf at Hershey's golf courses, you are helping to ensure that Milton S. Hershey's legacy will continue forever.

So why am I telling you all of this?

Before Tori was born, I worked at one of the museums on the Milton Hershey School campus, and my job was to teach visitors about life at the school as well as the history. One day it occurred to me that if Mr. and Mrs. Hershey had been able to have children of their own, it's very likely that MHS would not exist today and that tens of thousands of lives would never have been impacted. *What they initially thought was a tragedy turned into an incredible blessing.*

What a great example of God having plans far greater than we can possibly imagine.

I was reminded of this a couple of months after Tori's diagnosis, and I realized that it might possibly pertain to our own lives now.

That day, I wrote this:

> And I don't think I want God's greater plan. At this moment, I just want my Tori. A healed, typically developing Tori. I don't want God to use us without her. Rationally I know that this life is not my own, anyway. God alone knows why all of this is happening, and He can see the ending of our earthly story even though we can't. He knows the plans He has for us, with or without Tori.
>
> But that doesn't mean that I want that right now.
>
> This brings me back to a point of surrender, because I am reminded that God can redeem any circumstance we may encounter. He can take the tragic death of a child and make something beautiful from it.
>
> In the case of Mr. and Mrs. Hershey, their inability to have children of their own created an opportunity to touch tens of thousands of children.

> We continue to pray that Tori will be completely and miraculously healed here on this earth. That is our hearts' greatest desire.
>
> But if we have to lose Tori here on this earth, then I desperately want God to have a great plan for us, a purpose for her precious life . . . a plan far greater than we can imagine.

This struggle between our desires and God's plan would continue, and it forced me to daily surrender to His perfect will, even though I didn't fully understand it yet, and I may never.

24 God Is Always on Time

Background Music:
"Give Me Faith," by Elevation Worship

For most of Tori's life we were pondering her death. We wondered about the when, the how, the where. We maintained hope that she could still be fully healed; yet, as time passed, I found that I was struggling to pray for Tori's healing. I asked others to pray for it, but the words wouldn't form in my own heart and mind. I felt stuck, numb, defeated.

I absolutely wanted it and believed that it could happen, but I began to doubt that God would heal her here on earth. Because of this doubt, I struggled to pray. It is in times like this that I am most thankful that we don't have to pray with words. God knows our hearts, and His Word tells us that the Holy Spirit intercedes for us when we don't know what to say (Romans 8:26).

In retrospect, what I called doubt was likely the Holy Spirit gently preparing me for what was to come.

Hope is difficult. Hope requires a stamina and determination that can leave you feeling exhausted when you are already worn. I desperately wanted Tori to be healed on earth and couldn't think of anything I wanted more.

A friend had a dream in which I couldn't see an older, healed Tori in a picture on a wall. Tori was the older sibling to many children, and her testimony had changed the world. My friend could see Tori in the photograph, but I couldn't. This friend encouraged me to pray about the meaning and said this: that no matter what, I needed to see her as being healed, because she IS healed somewhere.

And we knew that. We did. But that didn't stop our minds from wandering and wondering. Would He heal Tori here on earth? If so, when and how? Gradual? Immediate? How much longer until the healing would happen? So much wondering, not enough trusting.

Though most of our interactions with others were positive, we had a few negative conversations that made us question our level of faith. Some said things like, "If you want God to heal Tori, you need to have more faith!" as if there is a scale of faith that God looks at as He makes His decision about whether or not to heal someone.

This became frustrating to me because I knew that God could heal her, but I also knew that He might choose not to do so here on earth. I was being realistic in my perspective and trusting the Lord with the outcome. Yet these few made me feel as though I had to live believing that He had already healed her on earth or it wasn't going to happen.

The God of the Bible is sovereign, omniscient, omnipotent, and omnipresent. He is not unjust in His decisions, and He isn't manipulated by our games. Brennan and I chose to surrender to His sovereign and wise plan instead of living a life that felt fake. After all, the climax to all of the best stories in the Bible start with "But God . . .," and we prayed that our story was one of those. "Krabbe was winning, but God . . ."

This is the meaning of true surrender, of total trust. I had no choice but to place Tori in HIS hands, because there is nothing on earth that could save her. But He could. Until His plan was revealed, we chose to love her fiercely and live life abundantly.

In our short life here on earth, we need to stop creating scenes in our head and instead trust the One who wrote the entire play. Whether He healed Tori here or in heaven, we knew He was going to heal her. She IS healed.

I reminded myself that this was only Act One and that Act Three is many pages away. We simply aren't meant to understand right now—we are meant to trust Him and keep on walking. Our God is never late. Our God loves us deeply and created us with purpose. And He is worthy of our complete trust, even in times like this.

Then like a hero who takes the stage when we're on
the edge of our seats saying it's too late.
—MERCYME, "FLAWLESS"

Genesis 1:1 says this: "*In the beginning God created the heavens and the earth.*" It's a verse we all probably know and yet how often do we ponder the wonder of these words?

To sum it up, God took nothing and made everything. He merely *spoke* and things like light, water, land, and everything else came into existence. He is powerful beyond imagination, and we were given the gift of the Bible so that we could know Him and love Him more.

For those of us who believe in God, who believe that the Bible is true, why is it so easy to believe that God can create the universe but so difficult to remember that He also loves us and is sovereign over our lives? I think that we can easily believe what the Bible says about the big things like Creation but not about the smaller things like our trials and tribulations because we don't consider ourselves worthy of His attention and care. Who are we that God would spend time caring for us?

If you've ever struggled with these feelings, consider what the Bible tells us about God's love for us:

John 3:16: "*For this is how God loved the world: He gave his one and only Son, so that everyone who believes in him will not perish but have eternal life.*"

Matthew 10:29–31: "*What is the price of two sparrows—one copper coin? But not a single sparrow can fall to the ground without your Father knowing it. And the very hairs on your head are all numbered. So don't be afraid; you are more valuable to God than a whole flock of sparrows.*"

Romans 8:35–38: "*Can anything ever separate us from Christ's love? Does it mean he no longer loves us if we have trouble or calamity, or are persecuted, or hungry, or destitute, or in danger, or threatened with death? (As the Scriptures say, "For your sake we are killed every day; we are being slaughtered like sheep.") No, despite all these things, overwhelming victory is ours through Christ, who loved us. And I am convinced that nothing can ever separate us from God's love. Neither death nor life, neither angels nor demons, neither our fears for today nor our worries about tomorrow—not even the powers of hell can separate us from God's love. No power in the sky above or in the earth below—indeed, nothing in all creation will ever be able to separate us from the love of God that is revealed in Christ Jesus our Lord.*"

Nothing can separate us from God's love. No matter what you may be experiencing in life, remind yourself of these truths (and so many more that I didn't list here) and remember that God loves you enough that He willingly gave His Son for you! He cares about you and He cares about what's happening in your life, more than you can ever imagine.

25 Security in the Mystery

Background Music:
"King of Love," by I Am They

*God is still good, sovereign, and faithful, despite the circumstances
we see around us, and is therefore worthy to be praised.*
—HEATHER ZEMPEL, *AMAZED AND CONFUSED*

I have found that God will often use a lesson or a specific Scripture passage that you read long ago but had forgotten; at just the right moment, He brings it to mind and speaks to you through it.

In September 2012, I had the privilege of hearing Beth Moore teach on 2 Kings 4:1–37 at a conference. Beth's teaching was relevant then, but it became even more relevant as we walked through this struggle with Tori's health.

One day, when I needed it most, my Bible reading for the day was on the same passage Beth had taught on years earlier! I remembered the conference and found my journal with the notes I had taken.

To summarize, 2 Kings 4:1–37 focuses on two women—one who is poor and has almost nothing, and one who is wealthy and has almost everything. Both have very different interactions with Elisha, the prophet.

The first woman has gone through much (the loss of her husband) and is now facing another tragedy (a creditor threatened to take her two sons away). She is honest about what she's going through and Elisha performs a miracle that allows her to keep her sons. The second woman says that she's perfectly fine when Elisha asks her what he can do for her, even though deep in her heart she has a longing that has not been fulfilled (the longing for a child).

The first woman is willing to ask for help and acknowledges her need. The second woman doesn't ask so that she will not be disappointed. Essentially, she says, "Don't mess with me," because she is so afraid that she will have her hopes dashed.

I am able to relate to the second woman and her struggles so well (aside from the wealthy part, though we have everything we need and more). My first thought when I read this was, "Wow—that's me." God changed my heart about being a mother when I least expected it; Brennan and I prayed and tried for a year and a half after that heart change before becoming pregnant. Those eighteen months brought monthly disappointments as we struggled to conceive. It became difficult to hope. I never took pregnancy tests, because I didn't want to see the negative result.

As I have said before, fear is easy, but hope is excruciating. Hope requires vulnerability and trust. Hope requires faith. Very few people knew we were trying to conceive; much like the second woman, I kept our struggles to myself because I didn't want to face our failure time and time again. I was "fine" on the outside.

When I took a pregnancy test on December 1, 2013, I couldn't believe my eyes. God had given us a child! My heart was so filled with joy during pregnancy (which I loved!) and even more so when Tori was born the following July. God so richly blessed us with her.

And on February 13, 2015, we found out He might be taking her away.

A few months postdiagnosis, I wrote this:

> It has been a tough six months since she became symptomatic, and an even tougher five months since she was diagnosed with Krabbe. And yet, our faith has only increased through this trial—not because we are certain that God will heal her here on earth, but because He has proven to us over and over again that He is good, He is faithful, He is trustworthy.
>
> Our desperation has brought us to a new place in our relationship with God and with each other. Do we understand why He has allowed this? No. Do we like it? Definitely not. But one thing remains true—He is loving and faithful! We choose to believe His Word and His

promises, no matter what. I don't know if our story will end up like this woman's story did, with her son being restored.

But I trust that God has only good things for us, even if we can't understand what is happening now.

Of all the things that Beth said that day, these points resonated with me the most:

1. Personal desperation can jar us out of secondhand stories. Don't live in someone else's story—get your own story. We were all meant to have our own miraculous story of how God has rescued and changed us. Our faith should be our own.

2. God didn't call us to "fine." He called us to faith. Do you want to live a life that is humanly explainable, or do you want to live a life in the supernatural provision of God? Your need is your invitation to supernatural provision! If you have everything you need, you need a bigger life (this does not contradict contentment). The woman doesn't ask so that she will not be disappointed. She wants to be safe. She lives a little life because she will not ask.

3. We are not called to a little life—we are called to an abundant life (John 10:10).
   Yet:
   a. We try to be faithful without the faith.
   b. We want to be safe; we want to be given something He won't take away.
   c. We choose to live a humanly explainable life to be comfortable.

> "Without faith it is impossible to please God." (Hebrews 11:6, NIV)

4. Faith trusts that every call to forsake is also a call to take. We forsake sin and take a life of peace and freedom. We forsake bitterness and take joy. We forsake fear and take courage. We are

called to participate, to act, in God's plan. Don't let people stand between you and Jesus. "Don't waste the harvest of failure. You will never have a better teacher."

5. Faith faces the fact that there is no formula. Formulas are our way of trying to control God. He knows we would go after the formula and results instead of the relationship.

6. Faith rests its case on the resurrection of the dead. There is nothing God cannot do.

Oh, my God, He will not delay, my refuge and strength always. I will not fear; His promise is true. My God will come through always!
—KRISTIAN STANFILL

Do I have enough security in God to trust Him with the mystery? To trust that He is good amid the waiting?

If God doesn't part your sea, He wants you to walk on it.
—BETH MOORE

26 What to Say (and What Not to Say) to Parents of a Dying Child

Background Music:
"Be Thou My Vision" (hymn)

When we made Tori's story public, we expected to hear from people genuinely trying to help save her life. We have greatly appreciated the time and energy people have put into trying to help her, and us! We wanted to share a few ideas of how to help families in need, as well as what we do not recommend based on our own experiences.

Though most of what we received was good, we also received messages and comments from people who clearly hadn't researched Krabbe and were merely trying to push their own beliefs and platforms on us. There is a huge difference between the two, and it is always obvious which camp the person is in. One woman offered "advice" to us that was completely irrelevant and didn't apply to Krabbe whatsoever; I politely declined her offer for a "miracle treatment" and thought we were finished.

If the issue had been left there, I wouldn't have minded. However, she posted the following status on her PUBLIC page not long after this conversation happened:

> It's surprising how quickly some dismiss what might save their life and the life of their child. The only thing you and I can do is to pray that their eyes, hearts, and minds will be open to exploring the truth. And to keep living the example. My heart breaks daily for so many people.

I was stunned when I saw this. The timing of it made it impossible to believe that it could be about anything—or anyone—else. I commented on her status, asking if she was writing in reference to me, and she promptly deleted my comment and the ones from other friends of mine who saw the post, and then deleted the post altogether and blocked all of us.

The whole situation made me laugh, honestly. Yes, I was annoyed when I saw her status about our conversation. How anyone could say something like that, claiming that we weren't doing everything we could to save our child's life, is unbelievable. But more than anything, I felt sorry for this woman. She was so misguided and didn't practice her own teachings about being open to the truth.

Krabbe is genetic. Nothing we did caused it.

Moral of the story: Don't say that parents of a dying child are not trying to save their child's life. Don't offer advice without researching the disease. It isn't helpful, it hurts feelings, and it wastes precious time.

Perhaps you have wondered how to best approach families in difficult situations. My friend Sharon Goldin has been living with chronically ill children for nearly twenty years now. She, more than anyone I personally know, can completely relate to our situation, and she offered helpful advice to me right after Tori was diagnosed. There's so much truth in what she shared, and since so many ask how they can help parents like us, I wanted to share her wisdom. Here are some of the suggestions Sharon offered of things that you should not say or do to a family with a special needs / chronically ill / terminally ill child:

- Don't commit to help and then bail. Remember that your friendship and support really matter—they may be a lifeline for your loved one. So, if you say you're going to help, commit to it. Having someone back out when your child is sick can be more devastating than you can imagine (trust me, I know this all too well firsthand—I lost way too many friends and learned who my "real" friends truly were).

- Don't visit without checking first, even if it's something you've planned with them in advance. One rough night can lead to a day of exhaustion for everyone, and they might not be up to visitors.
- Don't visit if you've recently been sick, feel like you may be getting sick, or if anyone else in your family is or has just been sick. Your germs can make someone with a weakened immune system very ill.
- Don't prolong the visit. Watch for cues from the parent or the child that it's time to wrap things up.
- Don't say, "God won't give you more than you can handle." It implies that God had a role in the child becoming ill and may make your friend feel as though he or she is being punished.
- Don't send latex balloons to the hospital. Many people are allergic to the latex in balloons and almost all children's hospitals are latex free.
- Don't send flowers. Sure, they're pretty, but the child won't care. Worse, if the child's immune system has been compromised, anything that could cause an allergic reaction or that carries bacteria could be life threatening.
- Don't take it personally if your friend doesn't want to talk. The stress of being a caregiver is overwhelming. Sometimes the best thing to do is just be there with your friend and let her vent, cry, or just sit in silence. Often your presence is enough.
- Don't be afraid to reach out with thoughtful phone calls or e-mails, but remember the family is likely overwhelmed and may not be able to respond. But know the thought is appreciated.
- Unless your child has the exact same diagnosis, don't give medical advice. You're not a doctor and you're certainly not familiar enough with the child's illness to be making medical calls. Unless you have a chronically ill child, you do not know how the parent is feeling. Unless you have been in the parents' shoes, do not say, "I know how you feel," as trust me, you do not. Do not say, "If you do this, it will cure your child! I know a parent whose kid was cured of cancer using this herb . . ." It is not helpful. The best advice you can give is offer to pray or help.

- Don't tell them to "chin up" or "cheer up." They are entitled to their feelings, which may or may not be comfortable for you.
- Don't tell horror stories and don't compare your friend's child to another who is seriously ill, too. It won't make anyone feel better. Your child having tubes in his ears or the flu is not the same as an incurable disease.
- Don't offer pity.
- The following phrases are not cool. Don't say:

  o "I know JUST how you feel." (No, you don't—unless you are in the same boat, and even then, EVERY child is different.)
  o "I feel helpless." (Imagine how your friend feels!)
  o "You need to talk about it." (NO, we don't—if we want to talk, we will.)
  o "Here! This is what you should do. I heard about it on *Oprah, Dr. Oz, The Doctors* . . ." (Who cares what they have to say? They are not my child's doctor.)
  o "I don't know how you're managing it all. I'd die if it were me." (Thoughtless! Again, it does not help. No, you would not die, and yes, you would be able to deal.)
  o "Everything is going to be fine." (You do not know that—and it's usually not true.)
  o "Everything happens for a reason."
  o "What's the life expectancy with that?" (Morbid!)

So, what should you do and/or say instead? According to Sharon:

- Do stay in touch: extended family and friends play an important and big role in helping children and their immediate families deal with a serious illness.
- Listen—really listen—to your friend or family member. It's important for people to tell their story—it helps them process traumatic situations. So let them talk and be a good listener.
- Send meals. Remember that while your friend or family member is in the hospital with their sick child, the food they have available is usually not great. Try to plan for fresh foods that are easy to

heat up and clean up, or failing that, have something delivered, like pizza or Chinese.

- If they have other children, offer to babysit during appointments or accompany them to the appointment if they need someone to sit with them.
- Be available to help out in the middle of the night for ER trips and other emergencies.
- Everyone wants to help immediately, but with a long-term illness, help will be needed all along the way. People get burned out easily, so spread the help out so you can be strong for them. Remember, your friend or family member will still need you in a month, three months, six months, even next year.
- Help set up a notebook or binder to keep important medical information in, or scan the documents for your friend or family member and put them in a file or flash drive. A copy of all the paperwork from discharges, diagnoses, and medication changes is so helpful and can be taken to all appointments or travels. If they're out of town and have to go to an ER or urgent care, they have all the information handy, and treatment is easier and safer.
- Learn about the disease their child is suffering from.
- Be calm and levelheaded for your friend, as at times they will not be able to think clearly, be it from stress or lack of sleep. It is okay to be upset, but it helps them if you're logical, orderly, and levelheaded. It's calming to them and helps them see things that they may not see otherwise.
- Offer to pick up medication at the pharmacy while you're out. If you're heading to the grocery store, call and see if they need anything.
- Gather folks to help clean and disinfect their home before they come back from the hospital, especially if there's been surgery.
- Offer to do an overnight stay and let them get some uninterrupted nighttime sleep. Sleeping in the day is fine, but there's nothing quite like a good six-hour stretch in the night to make a parent feel refreshed.
- Make a gift bag of disinfecting wipes, masks for the child when in public, soaps, and hand sanitizer. When dealing with sick kids,

you HAVE to be ultra clean all the time. A cold to you could mean death to a child with compromised immunity.

- Offer to help with the household chores or pet care. Offer to pay for a cleaning service or dog sitter/walker.
- Be willing to just sit in the waiting room with your friend. Just having another person present can be a huge stress reliever.
- If you're not local and want to help, gift cards are a great idea. Visa or AMEX gift cards can be used almost anywhere and are a good choice if you're unsure of what stores are local. Starbucks, Target, and Walmart gift cards as well as gas cards are also good bets. Mobile gift cards for apps on a smartphone are good, too. If the kid is older, a gift of puzzles, word games, and so forth is a great idea.
- Write your friend or family member a card to let them know you are thinking of them.
- Here are some things you can say that your friend or family member would appreciate:

  - "Do you need to talk / feel like talking? I'm here to listen."
  - "How are you / your child feeling today?"
  - Ask questions; remember the major issues and look them up—BUT do not offer suggestions for treatment.
  - Talk about care and hope. Talk about how sweet and precious their child is and how much you love them. You should validate the seriousness of the illness by confirming that they are facing something very difficult.
  - "I am heartbroken you and your baby are going through this. Hang in there and know there are so many people who care about you." Acknowledge that you know your friend or family member is in pain without saying you understand what they are going through.

Sharon's advice and support proved to be invaluable throughout our journey with Tori, and I am so thankful for her willingness to offer wisdom and advice even as she dealt with her own struggles and loss. Hopefully these tips will help you when you are faced with a friend or family member in a tough situation, as well.

27 Becoming Local Celebrities

Background Music:
"Flawless," by MercyMe

From our blog:

When I go to the dentist, I do not expect them to remember my name or who I am—after all, I am only there twice a year for less than an hour. However, today I struggle to find words to express how my visit to the dentist made me feel. The visit started as usual and the hygienist was making casual conversation with me. She then said, "I don't want to make you cry, but how is your daughter doing?" I stared at her blankly for a brief moment, trying to figure out how she could possibly know about Tori and how she could have made the connection that I am her mother.

Before I could say anything, she added, "One of the ladies in the office saw the article about your family in the paper and made sure that we all saw it."

I told her that Tori is doing fairly well and that I was amazed that she remembered the article (it was two months ago). I felt something I can't quite describe at that moment. My dentist's office (which is quite large and sees hundreds of people each year) remembered our names well enough to recognize them when they read them in an article two months ago. Brackbill is a common last name in Central Pennsylvania, so it wasn't the uniqueness of the name that enabled easy recognition. They remembered us for who we are.

And they remembered me today and asked about Tori. We have always had great experiences with this dental office, but today made me certain that this is where we should be going—they clearly care about their patients and take the time to know our names. And that seemingly little thing meant so much to me today.

This was only the beginning of our "local celebrity" status, as we jokingly called it. Because of Tori's presence in the news and her large following on Facebook, it became rare for us not to be recognized in public when we ventured out.

A few weeks after Tori's first birthday, I decided to start driving for Uber; I figured it would be good for me to get out of the house, and since I love driving, it was a perfect fit. I would go out and drive when Brennan was home in the evenings and on weekends—not every night, but as many as I could.

In early October I was out driving and picked up a gentleman from the Midtown area of Harrisburg and took him downtown. We talked a bit and then he received a phone call; while I tried not to eavesdrop, I heard him comment, "Well, that's life on the news." I gathered that he was somehow involved with the media, but I didn't get a chance to talk to him about it because we had arrived at his destination. He was kind and funny and I enjoyed our brief time together.

Later that month, I began asking Tori's Facebook supporters if they had any media contacts, because I wanted to get Krabbe back on the news. It didn't take long for our local CBS station to contact me; the man on the phone asked if he could come interview us in an hour! We quickly finished dinner, cleaned up the living room (but tried to make it look like we hadn't just frantically cleaned), and got ready to be on TV.

When the news crew arrived, I knew the reporter—Kyle Rogers— looked and sounded familiar. Since we rarely watch the news, I knew that wasn't it. I asked him if he uses Uber, and his eyes opened wide; he said, "I knew you looked familiar!" and we laughed about the "coincidence" of it all. But I knew that it was more than a coincidence—it was a divine appointment. God knew that Kyle would get into my van that night, and He knew that Kyle would be the one sent to our home to interview us about Tori.

The interview was shown twice that evening (it's amazing how quickly they put the pieces together!) and at every news time for the next four days. Kyle highlighted all that we had done with Tori and how we had chosen to live with joy instead of grief. Of course, we said far more than they actually broadcast, but that's to be expected.

During the interview, I made a point to discuss the legislation that had been signed into law in October 2014 that still hadn't been implemented; Kyle took that and ran with it and used his influence to put pressure on the Department of Health. While there were no immediate results, it was encouraging to see that we weren't the only ones who were frustrated that the state wasn't doing what it said it would do. Newborns were still not being screened for Krabbe, and we had a renewed fire within us to pursue this further.

CBS21 would end up doing three interviews with us—two with Kyle and one with Donna Kirker-Morgan—and we are so thankful for their care and support. After Tori passed away, Kyle came back over to speak with us and shared the story that evening on the news. He greeted us with hugs and asked us some great questions.

Thank you, Kyle, for helping Tori's voice be heard.

28 Hunter's Hope Symposium

Background Music:
"Good to Be Alive," by Jason Gray

When I was younger, my family had no loyalty to any particular teams. In baseball, we followed the career of my dad's friend, Dan Gladden, from the Giants to the Twins and finally the Tigers. We watched the 49ers for a little while because my dad enjoyed watching Joe Montana play, but we didn't really consider ourselves to be "fans" of any one team.

Another team we watched often was the Buffalo Bills. One of my mom's high school classmates, Gale Gilbert, was the backup quarterback for the Bills and went to four Super Bowls with them (never winning any). When you're from a small town, it's a big deal to have someone become "famous" in any respect.

We watched the Bills hoping to see Gale play, but he never got the opportunity because Jim Kelly, the starting quarterback, was that good. As a side note, Gale went on to play for the San Diego Chargers and went to a Super Bowl with them . . . and lost. He is known for being the only player in NFL history to have gone to five Super Bowls and yet to have never won a ring.

After Tori's diagnosis, we received many messages from her Facebook followers asking if we had heard about Hunter's Hope, which was started by Jim Kelly. His name wasn't immediately familiar to me, but it was to Brennan, my sports-loving husband.

People remembered the word Krabbe because of the advocacy of Jim and his family. The Kelly family lost their son, Hunter, to Krabbe in 2005, and they started a foundation in his honor to encourage leukodystrophy families and to advocate for newborn screening.

Each year the Hunter's Hope Foundation hosts a four-day event called the Family Symposium in Upstate New York. It is practically free for the families who attend and provides an incredible opportunity to be with others who completely understand what you have been through.

We wanted to attend but were unsure of how Tori would do on the drive since it was about five hours away from home. Brennan and I decided early on that renting a bigger vehicle was essential if we were going to attempt this drive, given the amount of stuff we would have to take. One thing that we learned quickly is that having a child with special needs requires a lot of stuff. A lot. Add in adaptive equipment and you are basically moving in wherever you go. We hoped that a newer, smoother car ride might help her be more comfortable, and it seemed to work. Tori slept pretty well, though she definitely had her moments of protesting. We had very few incidents and were so thankful.

Upon arrival, we got settled in and then headed down to the pool where we met some of the other families. Tori had never been in a pool before, so we were excited to try it! The pool was a little too chilly for her, so we tried the Jacuzzi next. It was warm, not hot. She loved that! After swimming we got cleaned up and headed down to the welcome dinner.

As we looked around at all of the families in attendance, a mix of emotions ran through our hearts. On one hand, it was amazing to be in a room where no one would be surprised by the sounds of a suction machine or feeding pumps, where we were normal for once; but it was also so heartbreaking to look around at all of those families who had terminally ill children (and those whose children had already passed) and recognize the pain that each and every person in that room had experienced or would experience.

Jim Kelly welcomed us all to the symposium and told his story about his son, Hunter. He talked about how his wife, Jill, is the one who told him that THIS was the perfect use for his fame: leukodystrophy awareness and action. His purpose was far greater than playing professional football! Indeed, their foundation has helped so many families! We had the opportunity to meet Jim and his family and I relayed the story about Gale to him and he laughed, saying that he had never heard that one before! He said that Gale was "one heck of a quarterback" and that he enjoyed being on a team with him. Jim Kelly is a class act.

Besides spending time with the other families, we also heard from several of the leading researchers and experts in Krabbe and other leukodystrophies. It was so informative and we feel so encouraged to know that such innovative, rigorous, and continuous research is being done to find a cure for the disease. No matter what cure may be found, early detection is still imperative.

One of the amazing things that was shared was this: some of the leukodystrophy researchers who work for Hunter's Hope were at our welcome dinner; as they saw all of us with our children and heard some of our stories, it apparently impacted them greatly. As with any career, you can become jaded and it can feel like just a job. Being with all of us increased their urgency to continue searching for a cure, better treatment, and so forth, because they realized that time doesn't just cost money, it costs lives. I am so thankful for the brilliant minds who are working so diligently to stop these diseases from taking more lives.

As I observed our leukodystrophy family that weekend, what impacted me more than anything was the love that radiated from each person.

Every one of us were in similar situations: our children were dying or had passed from horrific diseases. We were broken people, often unsure of what even the next hour might bring. Under these circumstances, you would expect to see constant tears, depression, sorrow, despondency. However, what we saw was the exact opposite.

These parents had chosen to make each day matter. They had chosen to make sure their child truly lived the fullest life possible. They chose joy. I loved watching the moms and dads with their children, showing such love, patience, devotion, and selflessness toward their precious gifts. Most of all, God used this time to show us that we would survive the death of Tori. We would be able to laugh again, smile again—we would be able to live.

I loved watching these moms and dads with the other affected children, because it was evident that they loved these children nearly as deeply as they loved their own. I especially loved watching the fathers—both with their babies and the babies who belonged to others. They loved holding them, talking to them, getting pictures taken with them, and loving them. They were so gentle and tender; they were completely involved in caring for the children they were holding, and the love that radiated from their faces was indescribable. The hardest part was not knowing if these children would be back the next summer. And yet, these fathers (and mothers) continued to embrace these children and love them freely.

There is beauty in the broken if you choose to look for it.

No parent chooses to have a child with special needs, but that shouldn't change how they love their child. The parents in our leukodystrophy community make a daily choice to love their children selflessly, joyfully, and abundantly. They choose to give their child the best possible life they can have. And they are an example we all should follow.

We have been so blessed and encouraged by being part of this community, and though we never would have chosen this, we are so thankful for every person we have met through our Krabbe journey and for the encouragement they provide to everyone else. None of us can do this on our own, so having support like this is invaluable, and it is vital.

Our trip to the symposium was enlightening in many ways, but what became most apparent was the need for a bigger vehicle in order to be able to transport Tori and her equipment. We had thought that Tori merely hated the car seat, but after renting the SUV for our trip to New York, it was clear that Tori had not been a huge fan of our Chevy Malibu. She loved the smooth ride of a bigger vehicle!

We had a considerable amount of money in our Team Tori account—money that had been donated to care for her. With that amount in mind, we began to search for a used minivan, and we found the perfect one! Without a doubt, that van became the single best investment we made with Tori's money. We could not have traveled with her as much as we did without the van. And she never cried in a vehicle again.

29 Tori's Bucket List

Background Music:
"Beautiful Day," by U2

When we got home from the symposium, it was time to celebrate Tori's first birthday and we decided to make it a momentous occasion since we were blessed that she was even turning one! We had family come in from all over the country and invited essentially everyone to join us for an afternoon of joy. The organization Icing Smiles made a beautiful cake for Tori at no cost, and we so appreciated this gift!

Her birthday party was just the beginning of the fun times to come. One of the observations we made at the symposium was that many families had created "bucket lists" for their children. It was something we had considered but had never really done. We wanted to do everything we could to help her "live" while she was alive:

> However, the knowledge that she's dying doesn't keep us from living in the moment and loving Tori fiercely and passionately today. That doesn't keep us home, afraid to leave the house. Rather, this has inspired us to fill her life with normal experiences that we would do with a healthy, typically developing child. To truly LIVE life with her by our side. Having a list of experiences to accomplish has filled our hearts with such joy and excitement. We are truly having an amazing time fulfilling each item on the list and creating memories. If God heals her in heaven, we will cherish these memories with her for the rest of our lives. And if God heals her on earth, we've simply got a head start on a lifetime of adventures and experiences to enjoy together. Unexpected circumstances can derail us or they can push us forward—it's a decision we have to make, daily. And we choose to live.

We decided to start a list of experiences we wanted Tori to have, and the list quickly grew. We shared the list with her Facebook followers and received not only additional items to add to the list, but also generous and unexpected donations toward completing those items! Her fans were so excited to help her have as many adventures as possible.

We added things to her list that every child should experience (playing in the leaves, feeding ducks, etc.) as well as things every person should try to experience (Disney World, Grand Canyon, etc.). The list ranged from the simple to the extravagant. We started on her first birthday by going to Build-A-Bear and catching fireflies. I faithfully blogged about each one, providing many pictures and details for our own benefit but also for those who were following her story.

Between July and December, we completed nearly fifty adventures, including Disney World (thanks to the Quinn Madeleine Foundation) and the Grand Canyon.

Here's the full list of Tori's completed adventures:

- Have a sleepover (07.11.15)
- Go to Build-A-Bear (07.30.15)
- Catch fireflies (07.30.15)
- Finger paint something for Mommy and Daddy (07.31.15)
- Have a picnic at Lake Tobias (08.01.15)
- See the butterflies at the Hershey Gardens (08.14.15)
- Ride on the *Pride of the Susquehanna* Riverboat (08.14.15)
- Float on a raft down a river (08.21.15)
- Feed ducks (08.21.15)
- Attend a Harrisburg Senators game (08.21.15)
- Go to the zoo (08.27.15)
- Feed giraffes (09.04.15 and 11.01.15)
- Go to the beach / build a sand castle (09.05.15)
- Watch the sunrise over the Atlantic (09.06.15)
- Go to a Phillies game (09.11.15)
- Visit the Statue of Liberty and NYC and take the Staten Island Ferry (09.12.15)
- Visit Disney World (09.15.15–09.17.15)
- Go to the National Aquarium in Baltimore (09.19.15)
- Kayak down a river (09.25.15)
- See Mommy's college—APU (10.09.15)
- Visit Disneyland (10.10.15)
- See the Grand Canyon (10.11.15)
- See a giant cactus (10.13.15)
- Meet my (Tori's) great-great-grandmother (10.15.15)
- Meet radio personality Brant Hansen (10.25.15)
- Go to a pumpkin patch (10.24.15 and 10.25.15)
- Play in the leaves (10.30.15)
- See daddy's college (PSU) and go to a football game (10.31.15)
- Meet Bumper the Seal at Hersheypark (11.06.15)

- See a real fire truck (11.11.15)
- See real reindeer at Hersheypark (11.14.15)
- Get a pedicure with Mama (11.27.15)
- Ride "Santa's Surprise Train" (11.28.15)
- Cut our own Christmas tree (11.29.15)
- Decorate our Christmas tree (11.29.15)
- Be a bridesmaid (12.05.15)
- Go to a Hershey Bears hockey game and meet Coco the mascot (12.06.15)
- See the Hotel Hershey's Christmas tree (12.07.15)
- Attend a Philadelphia Flyers game (12.08.15)
- Make a gingerbread house (12.16.15)
- Get a picture with Santa (12.27.15)
- Get a picture by the "Victoria Avenue" sign (12.27.15)
- Build a snowman (01.24.16)
- Join a hockey team (01.30.16)
- Wear Mama's wedding dress (02.08.16)
- Attend a tea party (03.10.16)
- Jump in a puddle (03.25.16)
- Find Easter eggs (03.25.16)
- Meet an NFL football player: Jordan Hill from the Seattle Seahawks, at our home (04.12.16—completed by Mommy and Daddy)
- Visit other states (fifteen of them: PA, CA, MD, NY, NJ, FL, OH, AZ, DE, CT, RI, MA, ME, NH, and VT)
- Fly on an airplane (twenty-two times!)

We always chose adventures that would stimulate her in some way while also providing a wide variety of experiences for her. More than anything, the bucket list helped us maintain a focus on living with Tori while she was with us, creating priceless memories and filling photo albums with these joy-filled photos along the way.

While each of these was memorable and I could write so much about them, I am only going to highlight a couple from the list. The sunrise over the Atlantic is one of my favorites because we were amazed at Tori's reaction. We were staying at my friends Alex and Rachael's condo in

Wildwood Crest for the weekend to fulfill some of the beach-related adventures, and we weren't sure if she would even care about the sunrise; but she did. Her eyes were alert and she never stopped looking at the colors of the sky as the sun rose over the horizon. So worth the very early wake up.

Another special memory was having the opportunity to meet our favorite radio personality. When I first moved to Pennsylvania, I discovered a wonderful human named Brant Hansen. Brant has many talents, and my first encounter was his morning show on our local Word FM station that almost made me enjoy mornings. Almost. It definitely made our early-marriage commute to work much more enjoyable!

In the years since, we have come to appreciate Brant for so much more. He is a passionate spokesperson for CURE International, he loves Jesus and challenges us to think about things in different ways, he wrote an incredible book called *Unoffendable* (which is also so challenging), and he's funny. Truly hilarious at times.

We have Word FM on constantly at home, so we hear Brant's show daily (it's now in the afternoon). It's often a topic of conversation in our home, and we are so thankful for him. So once we found out that he and his wife were moving to Harrisburg so that he could work for CURE, we were so excited. We added "meet radio personality Brant Hansen" to Tori's list not thinking that it was very likely to happen . . . until our pastor told us that Brant would be speaking at our church—Transcend Church—that October!

I wrote to Brant earlier that week to introduce our family and tell him briefly about Tori so that we could avoid small talk (something neither Brant nor I enjoy) and so that he was aware of her bucket list (and his presence on it). He replied the next day and said he looked forward to meeting Tori!

Brant came over to us briefly before church started and then again afterward to talk to us and Tori. He talked to Tori about her giraffe, her headband, and many other things, spending at least ten minutes with her. His kindness meant so much to us. Tori truly seemed to recognize his voice and her eyes got big while he talked. Since he was on the radio every weekday in our house or car, it made sense that she would know his voice!

Brant further surprised us that week by posting on his Facebook page about Tori *and* by speaking about her on his radio show! Here's what he said:

> This was a big deal: I got to meet one of our tiniest listeners this week. Her name's Tori: she is teeny tiny, a year old. And they don't think she's going to live to be two—she has a terminal genetic disease. She actually has ten thousand-plus followers on Facebook, which is amazing because it's really her parents' story. They have a bucket list for Tori—they love her dearly, and they just have things they want her to do, so they've been

checking things off the list. I was honored to be on the list, to get to meet her. To her, who knows, but she did seem to recognize my voice. They say they keep it the radio on all the time. And that was sweet. But I got to sit next to her and she's adorable, oh my goodness. What an honor.

I want to mention it, because frankly, I'm honored to be her adult friend person, but also, if you're interested in following her story . . . her parents are really inspiring. I got to meet them, and really love them. How they're dealing with knowing what's happening with their daughter, that she's terminal. And how they see God in this. Because I think a lot of us wonder, What if the worst possible thing happened? And for those of us who are parents, we know what that is, and it's interesting to see how God shows up when the worst possible thing happens. It's Team Tori on Facebook. What a sweetie: that was one of my highest honors—to get to kneel down by her little stroller there . . .

We were so honored that Brant was so willing to interact with Tori, and we loved seeing her eyes get big while he spoke to her. We saw Brant and met Sherri—the show's producer—only a month before Tori went to heaven, and she got to see his studio and deliver California almonds to him. Thank you, Brant, for loving our Tori.

If you want to learn more about each individual adventure and check out the pictures, visit our blog at www.thebrackbills.com.

Tori did more in her mere twenty months of age than some people do in a lifetime, and we hope and pray that she enjoyed these experiences as much as we did. Perhaps she's telling everyone in heaven all about the adventures that her mama and daddy took her on while she was on earth. I can't wait to hear her perspective.

30 Joy Rediscovered

Background Music:
"Nothing Is Wasted," by Jason Gray

After the first month of living in our new normal, Brennan and I decided that we weren't going to live out the remainder of Tori's days in grief and sadness. She didn't deserve miserable parents—she deserved to have the best possible life we could give her. We made the decision that we weren't going to mourn while she was still with us (Ecclesiastes 3); instead, we were going to choose JOY.

This wasn't a coping mechanism, nor was it a form of denial. Amidst the sorrow, we chose early on to love her fiercely and to LIVE while she was with us here on earth.

Inspired by other Krabbe families, we shared Tori's adventures on the blog and on her Facebook page. Tori's followers loved the adventures we had with her and frequently commented on our blog posts. The comment repeated the most was that we were always smiling in our pictures. That people pointed this out has always surprised me, and here's why:

Tori was here. Tori was cognitively aware. Tori was healthy (Krabbe aside). We had so much to be thankful for despite the looming threat of death that was constantly present. By making memories with her and sharing her with our families and friends, we recognized that there was a time to laugh, a time to dance, a time to live.

We knew that death would likely come far too soon for our precious daughter, and when that time came, we would mourn and grieve, but not while she was alive and well. At the same time, the mix of emotions as we lived out each day is difficult to describe. Our adventures were so fun and filled our hearts with such joy. We felt like a "normal family" doing normal things, and the diversions were refreshing.

Photo by Nicole Benner of Reflective Light Photography

Yet there were moments during our adventures when I was speechless, filled with emotion. I was saddened by the knowledge that we shouldn't have to have a bucket list for our baby; I was heartbroken by the realization of all that she wouldn't be able to do and experience some day.

One example happened at our cousin's wedding; it was so beautiful and perfect, so filled with joy. But when the bride danced with her father during the reception, my heart ached for Brennan, because we knew that without a miracle, he wouldn't get to walk Tori down the aisle someday and dance that special father-daughter dance with her.

He and I looked at each other later that same evening and I told him that being there was harder on me than I had expected, and he replied, "I know." Without speaking details, we knew we were on the same page.

The joy didn't replace the heartache; rather, they tensely coexisted each day, fighting for our undivided attention.

When I looked at Tori's beautiful face as I watched her fight this horrific disease, my heart swelled with fierce love and admiration. She was perfect, beautiful, smart, and gentle. She was so precious to us. She was God's gift to us, and she deserved our joy, our love, and our attention.

The time for mourning and grieving would come. Eventually. Until then, it was a time for joy, for laughter, for dancing, for life, and for love.

As parents you are excited when your children achieve new milestones or learn new things. With Tori, the bar was lowered drastically as time passed. When she would swallow occasionally, we would praise her. When she would try to make noise, we would applaud. We always sought to find a reason to tell her "good job" or some other phrase of praise just in case she was aware enough to feel good about her accomplishments.

It was in those moments that I often felt pangs of grief, of despair. She should be doing so much more. She should be able to express herself. She should . . . but Krabbe . . .

Krabbe is ruthless and cruel, slowly (yet at times, rapidly) robbing its victims of even the simplest of abilities, like breathing, swallowing, seeing, moving, eating.

How much did Tori know? How frustrated was she with her body? Did she remember that she used to be able to laugh? Smile? Move and wiggle? Eat real food?

The normal parenting experience doesn't—and shouldn't—involve suctioning your baby so her own saliva doesn't create pneumonia; listening to the beeping of a pulse oximeter and watching the numbers constantly; adjusting oxygen flow; using a feeding pump to provide nourishment; or making funeral and burial arrangements.

Each day was a careful balance between that reality—that things weren't as they should be—and the reality we chose: one of joy and appreciation for every moment, despite the hand we had been dealt.

When our reality became too much on any given day, we would switch our perspective and remember that we had much for which to be thankful. Having cultivated the discipline of gratitude for years coupled with our belief in God's faithfulness is what brought us joy and peace, even in the shadow of death.

*Even when I walk through the darkest valley, I will
not be afraid, for you are close beside me.
Your rod and your staff protect and comfort me.*
—PSALM 23:4

When we saw healthy babies, we realized that we were amazed by all that they could do, the little things like holding their heads up, grabbing toys, squirming to break free. These typical baby actions became a wonderful experience for us.

That made me realize that Krabbe didn't steal my joy: it increased it. It made it more sensitive and amplified it.

31 "Do You Ever Tell God that You Are Angry at Him?"

Background Music:
"Once and for All," by Chris Tomlin

"My thoughts are nothing like your thoughts," says the LORD.
"And my ways are far beyond anything you could imagine."
—ISAIAH 55:8

Early on, we were asked often if we were angry at God or frustrated with Him. We could—and can—honestly say no, we were not. Are we curious to know why this happened? Of course. Do we have our moments of sorrow and frustration at our circumstances? Definitely. But anger at God has not been and is not currently something we are experiencing. God is God and we are not.

Though we have our moments where we have to refocus our thoughts and remind ourselves of God's character, Brennan and I trust God completely; even though we don't like what has happened, we know that we will eventually (even if in heaven) understand why this happened. We know beyond any doubt that God is trustworthy, faithful, and loving. We know that He will be glorified through Tori's life.

This doesn't mean that we are "okay" with the situation, blindly accepting it without emotion. But it does mean that it's "okay" in the sense that we know that God is in control, we know that He loves us—and Tori—and we know that He has an amazing plan for all of our lives. We are unable to comprehend His plan at this moment, but we trust that He has one.

147

From soon after diagnosis until now, we have been filled with His peace that exceeds all that we understand (Philippians 4:7). There is no earthly reason for us to be so at peace with all of this—it is absolutely from God. We are able to be at peace because we trust the One who knows all and created all. We trust Him fully with our precious Tori and know that He loves her even more than we do. We know that He eventually uses all things for the good of those who love Him (Romans 8:28).

We were also comforted by having a clear understanding of death and heaven. Knowing what was in store for her should God choose to not heal her here on earth brought peace and comfort as we watched her earthly shell deteriorate.

It was a moment-by-moment process of surrendering all of this to Him and choosing to not worry, to not be angry, and to continue to hope that He would choose to heal Tori here on earth. We knew that He is more than able, and nothing is impossible for Him (Luke 1:37)!

On the day of Tori's surgery to have her G tube placed, Brennan and I sat in the waiting room and filled our time with reading and praying, among other things. I had brought my Bible along and the reading for that day was from Psalm 66:1–12, 16–20. It couldn't have been more perfect:

Shout joyful praises to God, all the earth!
Sing about the glory of his name! Tell the world how glorious he is.
Say to God, "How awesome are your deeds! Your
enemies cringe before your mighty power.
Everything on earth will worship you; they will sing your
praises, shouting your name in glorious songs."
Come and see what our God has done, what
awesome miracles he performs for people!
He made a dry path through the Red Sea, and his people went across on
foot. There we rejoiced in him. For by his great power he rules forever.
He watches every movement of the nations; let no rebel rise in defiance.
Let the whole world bless our God and loudly sing his praises.
Our lives are in his hands, and he keeps our feet from stumbling.

You have tested us, O God; you have purified us like silver.
You captured us in your net and laid the burden of slavery on our backs.
Then you put a leader over us.
We went through fire and flood, but you brought
us to a place of great abundance. . . .
Come and listen, all you who fear God, and
I will tell you what he did for me.
For I cried out to him for help, praising him as I spoke. If I
had not confessed the sin in my heart, the Lord would not have
listened. But God did listen! He paid attention to my prayer.
Praise God, who did not ignore my prayer or
withdraw his unfailing love from me.

Yes, praise God who does not ignore our prayers or withdraw His unfailing love from us.

32 *What Will Never Be*

Background Music:
"Help Me Find It," by Sidewalk Prophets

*When a sickness takes my child away and there's nothing
I can do, my only hope is to trust in You.*
—RYAN STEVENSON, "EYE OF THE STORM"

My heart officially broke on diagnosis day. Shattered, really. As time progressed, it was as if I had used superglue to temporarily mend the damage. It was a quick fix so that I could survive what was to come and to live while Tori was alive.

But situations like this are brutal. You know death is inevitable, but you have to wait. You are given a general guideline of what to expect but it isn't an absolute. So you walk along with a superglued heart, knowing that it will be broken again when your child actually passes away.

The healing can't begin until the second break occurs. Until then, your heart is damaged, hurting, longing for the suffering to be over—both for your child and for you as parents—but also never wanting to let your child go.

♡

*All of my life, in every season, You are still God; I have
a reason to sing, I have a reason to worship.*
—HILLSONG, "THE DESERT SONG"

Today has been one of those days where even looking at Tori as I hold her makes my heart break.

I study every detail of her perfect, beautiful face so that I can never forget her features. I gaze into her stunningly gorgeous eyes and plead with God to let me look into them for the rest of my life. I hold her tightly, hoping that I can hold onto her forever.

I beg Him to restore her, to remove this horrific disease from her body and heal her brain. In desperation, I cling to her and try to savor every moment, knowing that there may come a day when I cannot hold her any longer.

And strangely, it is in those moments of desperation that I find it easiest to pray.

Often, during daily life with Tori, I am left speechless, unable to pray for my precious daughter. Words fail my broken heart and in those moments I am so thankful that not only are tens of thousands praying for Tori, but the Bible tells us that the Holy Spirit intercedes for us (Romans 8:26) when we don't know what to pray.

I cannot imagine losing her, even though I know that without God's intervention, we will. Medically speaking, it is a fact.

But I also know that we serve a mighty God, a God who raised people from the dead and healed the sick. The same God who created everything in the universe loves me, loves Brennan, loves Tori. He spoke the universe into existence and there is nothing He cannot do!

Nothing can separate us from His amazing love. Even when we don't understand His plan or why He is allowing things to happen, we can rest assured knowing that His love for us is unending!

The joy we have because of the love of Jesus (and the love He is showing us through all of you) eases our pain and allows us to smile and make the most of our time with Tori. Both the joy we experience and the grief and pain that creep into our hearts at times leave us speechless, and it is then that we feel the Lords presence the most.

And the Holy Spirit helps us in our weakness. For example, we don't know what God wants us to pray for. But the Holy Spirit prays for us with groanings that cannot be expressed in words. And the Father who knows all hearts knows what the Spirit is saying, for the Spirit pleads for us believers in harmony with God's own will. And we know that God causes everything to work together for the good of those who love God and are called according to his purpose for them. . . . And I am convinced that nothing can ever separate us from God's love. Neither death nor life, neither angels nor demons, neither our fears for today nor our worries about tomorrow—not even the powers of hell can separate us from God's love. No power in the sky above or in the earth below—indeed, nothing in all creation will ever be able to separate us from the love of God that is revealed in Christ Jesus our Lord.
(ROMANS 8:26–28, 38–39)

Brennan and I did mostly well with our reality regarding Tori. I'm not usually a very emotional woman, so it became fairly easy to adjust to my new normal and get through daily life with Tori, even if I was numb some days. Since we were around Tori far more than we were around other babies, it also made it fairly easy to forget that she was so sick. She was our "normal" and we forgot that she really wasn't.

We did our best to not focus on what she couldn't do; instead, we celebrated and cherished every positive thing, every moment that God gave us with her.

Despite our decision to not be miserable and to make the most out of this situation, there were times when we were reminded that Tori was anything but "normal," and those moments were sometimes difficult.

We had a few local friends with babies who were within a month of

Tori's age, and there were times when we saw them and were reminded of the severity of our situation. We did not resent those friends or feel sorry for ourselves when we were with them (nor did we want anyone to feel sorry for us). Instead, we decided to celebrate with those friends because babies/children are a blessing and a joy and their milestones should be celebrated and remembered. We didn't wish our situation on ANYONE.

But it was in those moments that we were reminded not only of all that Tori couldn't do, but also of the fact that without a miracle, she would never do what those babies were doing. It is an odd feeling to be simultaneously excited for others but also deeply hurting for your own situation.

On one of those days, I wrote the following:

> Then the pain returns . . . an indescribable feeling of painful desperation, willing with everything within me for the situation to change and for everything to be fine. For Tori to be crawling, getting into everything, teething, learning. For Tori to grow and become a beautiful woman. For me to be able to be not only a mother, but Tori's mother. Forever.
>
> Then I think about the fact that I may never be pregnant again. I think about how desperately I wanted to be pregnant with Tori for those eighteen months of trying . . . how elated we were to finally conceive . . . how much I loved the experience of being pregnant . . . and now those feelings are sharply contrasted with the fear and grief of knowing that getting pregnant again is a huge risk . . . of being unsure that we even want to have (or obtain) any more children if we lose Tori.
>
> In those moments, I cry out to the Lord for mercy, for peace that surpasses understanding, for clear direction and wisdom, for a miracle that can only be attributed to HIM. Those moments awaken my emotions for Tori, Krabbe, and her future, and I am reminded of the severity of our situation and of our helplessness without the Lord. It is hard to describe the

hurt, but it is something that I physically feel in those moments.

We don't hide from the pain—hiding doesn't bring healing (for ourselves or for Tori). Thankfully, we do well most days and these moments of pain and mourning are infrequent for the time being. And we don't seclude ourselves from our friends and their children. Instead, we choose to love those children and be excited as we watch them grow and develop normally.

Just because our baby is sick doesn't mean that we should be bitter and angry about healthy children.

It's best to just focus on today, to focus on how well Tori is doing despite her circumstances. Thinking about the future only brings pain that isn't meant for today. If Jesus takes her home, we will certainly grieve then, but we will also rejoice because she won't be suffering any longer. We will rejoice that her little life has impacted so many, including our own. And most of all, we will rejoice because she is made perfect in heaven and will be there to meet us someday.

We know that we will be tempted to feel sorry for ourselves or to be jealous of others with healthy children for the rest of our lives, but we will focus on what we have and not what we don't have. We will praise the God who gave us Tori even though He took her to heaven so soon. And we will celebrate our friends' children even if we aren't blessed with any more of our own. It's just the way it should be.

The words of Alfred Lord Tennyson have wandered around in my mind ever since we received Tori's diagnosis:

'Tis better to have loved and lost / Than never to have loved at all.

I have pondered his words over and over again, and it took me a long time to be able to agree with him. I considered only the pain that would come if we lost her, the depth of the hurt from having to say good-bye. I knew that to lose her would hurt more than we could begin to imagine at the time. I tried to move past the present pain to consider these things: Would the pain we experienced be worth the immense love we feel for her? Would it be worth the joy she has brought to our lives?

Now, on this side of the story, I can definitively say yes, it was and is worth it all. Her presence changed us. It drew us closer to each other and to the Lord. Loving her even though she was only in our arms for twenty months was worth every tear.

33 *Grief and Resentment*

Background Music:
"Great Is Thy Faithfulness" (hymn)

This is the message you have heard from the
beginning: We should love one another.
—1 JOHN 3:11

After Tori's diagnosis was given, I became more aware of those in my life who had also lost children, though in different circumstances. Some had dealt with it well and were able to remember their child with joy and function normally. Others never dealt with the grief and can no longer function well. I knew I didn't want to be like the latter.

It sounds like a contradiction—to be grieving and choose joy—but it truly wasn't.

I also knew that Tori was aware of my emotions, so I decided to do my best to be joyful around her. I spoke to her lovingly and happily, never knowing how much she could understand but wanting her to feel loved always.

Brennan and I quickly found that we were dealing with Tori's diagnosis similarly, and we were grateful for that as we knew that would make things a bit easier as time passed and Tori's condition worsened. We continued to be open and honest with each other on the rough days, especially if we felt frustrated with one another because we recognized that the root of the annoyance was usually grief, and not the action of the other person. Our marriage grew even stronger—and that was purposeful. We learned to show extra grace and patience with each other as we navigated these new waters.

That was not the case, however, for everyone in our life.

Not only did we have to deal with the emotional impact of being parents to a child with a terminal diagnosis, but we had to deal with those who freaked out and took their grief out on us in some hurtful ways. We had heard stories from many other families regarding how those closest to them dealt with their child's diagnosis but never dreamed that anyone in our lives would not take it well—or that they would take it out on us. But it happened, and it was horribly hurtful and confusing. The public and private attacks came out of nowhere at the time we needed their support the most.

And the truth is that we did nothing wrong. We are by no means perfect, and we certainly do not do everything right all the time. But it became apparent down the road that we were merely the final straw for those involved, as they had their own issues that they had suppressed and they didn't know how to deal with them properly. Tori's diagnosis was simply too painful for them to handle in addition to the pain they carried from their past. What makes us the saddest is that those involved only saw Tori a handful of times despite their geographical proximity to us. They made the choice to stay away, one that they will likely regret later.

Out of respect for those involved, we will not provide specific details. However, we felt it was important to address this issue because many other Krabbe families expressed similar situations in their own lives, as well. We were blindsided by what happened to us, so it is important that I include this here.

If you have a child with a terminal diagnosis or even a chronic illness, be prepared to be treated differently by those closest to you. While we hope that anyone in our shoes will NOT encounter a situation like we did, it seems that it is very common, and I want to prepare you.

On the other hand, if you are tempted to be mean or take out your own emotions on the parents of a terminally ill child, I offer this: Don't allow grief to sabotage your remaining relationships. Put yourself in their shoes and don't unleash your frustration in hurtful ways.

It was through this situation that we learned a great deal about how to show grace, even in the midst of pain. It's been said that trials bring out your true character, and I admit that I was surprised at who I became throughout this journey.

Before Tori's diagnosis, I wasn't always happy with who I had become. We had many unexpected changes in the year prior to her birth; some had hardened my heart and left me bitter and unable to show grace easily. Add sleep deprivation into the mix and you have the perfect storm. These were mostly internal struggles—on the outside, I was able to keep everything normal and in control.

I found that it was easy for bitterness to creep back into my heart as we encountered negativity from those closest to us in response to Tori's diagnosis. Brennan said it so well: *"I wish people could see exactly what I, Lesa, and other Krabbe families go through on a daily basis. Maybe then we would be offered a little grace for our shortcomings and oversights. And yes, that includes forgiving ourselves for the mistakes we make, especially with Tori."*

Brennan and I had to continually refocus our hearts and minds on Scripture in order to keep bitterness and resentment away. One of those verses was 2 John 1:6:

> *Love means doing what God has commanded us,*
> *and he has commanded us to love one another,*
> *just as you heard from the beginning.*

We are told as Christians to do two things: love God and love others. By focusing on those two things, we will end up obeying the law of God and the law of man without even realizing it most of the time. There are many things that can hinder us from fulfilling this command, many things that can negatively affect our perspective and perception of others without us realizing it.

Similarly, forming a first impression of someone happens automatically. You meet someone, and based on the first few minutes of your interaction, you form an opinion. Those first few moments do not provide full insight into a person's context, character, or true self. You merely catch a glimpse instead of knowing and understanding them fully. Once an impression is formed, overcoming that perspective can be difficult no matter what experience may prove to be the truth.

In photography, the lens is how you see the world. The quality and integrity of the lens is crucial. Everything depends on the lens, even the quality of the final image. If your lens is cracked, smudged, or otherwise compromised, your image will be unclear or even indistinguishable from the view/reality you saw with your eyes; your perspective will not translate into a beautiful finished image like you had planned. It will be distorted. You will be disappointed, possibly angry, and unfulfilled. There was nothing wrong with the subject you were attempting to photograph, but the lens made it appear to be flawed.

I mention these things because I have been pondering what the Bible has to say about bitterness, anger, resentment, and how those things affect our perception of people and circumstances. When we hold grudges and harbor bitterness, anything the "guilty" person says or does will be viewed through a cracked lens. You will question their motives even if they are being kind. If we aren't loving people as God commanded us to do, the perspective will be skewed, and the relationship may be further damaged because we aren't seeing things clearly.

Perhaps this is why Jesus told us to resolve our issues with people directly and promptly (Matthew 18); to get rid of all anger and bitterness (Ephesians 4:31); and to get rid of the plank in our own eyes before judging the splinter in the eyes of others (Matthew 7:3–5). With bitterness, anger, and resentment in our heart, our lens is cracked and we cannot perceive the actions and words of people correctly and therefore cannot love them as we are commanded. We cannot fulfill our mission.

> *Your love for one another will prove to the*
> *world that you are my disciples.*
> —JOHN 13:35

Resentment is a dangerous thing. Many times in my life I have seen the aftermath of built-up resentment that was never resolved biblically. It has split churches, destroyed friendships, and created friction in families. Someone can do something or say something to you with great intentions, but because you are harboring unspoken resentment and bitterness, you read between the lines in order to justify your feelings. We've all done it! Rather than going to the person as soon as the alleged offense occurs to find out their true intent and to clear up misunderstandings, we choose to remain silent and allow bitterness to eat away at our heart, all while pretending that everything is fine on the outside.

Pride is an equally dangerous companion to resentment. This is a human flaw that we all deal with at some point in our lives, and that's exactly why Jesus spoke about this issue in Matthew 18:

> "If another believer sins against you, go privately and point out the offense. If the other person listens and confesses it, you have won that person back. But if you are unsuccessful, take one or two others with you and go back again, so that everything you say may be confirmed by two or three witnesses. If the person still refuses to listen, take your case to the church. Then if he or she won't accept the church's decision, treat that person as a pagan or a corrupt tax collector." (15–17)

Don't let bitterness, resentment, anger, or irritation destroy you. Don't let them destroy relationships or communities. The enemy LOVES when Christians do this! Don't let him have the satisfaction. There are so many verses that tell us to not be bitter or resentful, but to love; here are a few:

> Make every effort to keep yourselves united in the Spirit, binding yourselves together with peace. (Ephesians 4:3)
>
> And so, dear friends, while you are waiting for these things to happen, make every effort to be found living peaceful lives that are pure and blameless in his sight. (2 Peter 3:14)
>
> But we don't need to write to you about the importance of loving each other, for God himself has taught you to love one another. (1 Thessalonians 4:9)
>
> Get rid of all bitterness, rage, anger, harsh words, and slander, as well as all types of evil behavior. Instead, be kind to each other,

> *tenderhearted, forgiving one another, just as God through Christ has forgiven you. (Ephesians 4:31–32)*
>
> *Fools vent their anger, but the wise quietly hold it back. (Proverbs 29:11)*
>
> *And this is his commandment: We must believe in the name of his Son, Jesus Christ, and love one another, just as he commanded us. (1 John 3:23)*

I strive to take the following steps whenever I am in situations where I am hurt, and I do my best to not assume anything about the person. These have helped me tremendously, and I hope they are useful to you as well:

- Consider the context: What is the person going through? If you don't know, then offer grace and understanding instead of becoming angry immediately. Ask questions instead of assuming.
- Remember that no one is perfect, including you.
- Think about the true cause of the offense: Why is it bothering you? Was your pride hurt?
- Always assume the best about the people you love and not the worst.
- Communicate! In person is the BEST way to do this, but if the other party won't consent to doing so, make your written communication clear and your emotions known, remembering that words are powerful. Text leaves so much to the imagination, and it can often make issues far worse than they were at the beginning.
- Talk about things immediately; don't blindside someone years later.
- Make the effort to humbly make things right. Put aside your pride. Don't allow misunderstandings and misperceptions to destroy relationships. Life is too short and too precious to allow bitterness and resentment to steal our joy.

We are here on earth to love one another, to encourage, to build up, to lead others to Christ. Resentment prevents us from fully loving God and others, and it lets the enemy win. Choose love, choose joy, choose humility. It's worth it.

34 Parenthood and the Unexpected

Background Music:
"King of My Heart," by Kutless

I wanted to include some of the posts I wrote about the unexpected path our lives have taken. As I rocked Tori I would think about many things, but one frequent thought was about our unmet expectations:

> Brennan and I never expected our lives as parents to go this way—who does? No one has a child expecting to only have them for a few years and then lose them. Parenthood is supposed to be a lifelong adventure. This is not normal. And yet, that is where we potentially are, defying the natural order of the way things should be according to God's plan.
>
> We are stuck in a waiting game; waiting for a miracle that may not come; waiting (and dreading) for her to pass; waiting for the disease to progress (while hoping for improvement with every test); waiting to see the purpose of it all. Waiting.
>
> Waiting is terribly difficult no matter the circumstances; but in the case of families like us, this waiting is the worst possible kind. We are told the average life expectancy and live each day aware of the potential remaining months of our child's life, but also know that some exceed that expectancy. We make long-term plans knowing that we might have to break

them; or, we hesitate to plan anything more than two weeks out, because we just don't know. We wait.

We don't know what tomorrow holds—no one does. But our circumstances seem different than most. We know that a tomorrow looms ominously ahead where, without a miracle, our Tori will leave us far too soon. We don't know what that will look like, but we have an idea because of those who have passed before. It is a struggle between wanting to keep her here every possible second but also wanting her to be free from Krabbe and to join Jesus in heaven as soon as possible so that she doesn't suffer any longer. This isn't what parenthood should be about.

Two of the areas of our home that made me sad were her playroom and her bedroom:

Her toys sit where they were first placed one year ago, nearly untouched and gathering layers of dust.

The special place in the basement that we created for her playtime, learning, and general enjoyment has yet to be used by Tori.

One year ago, as we began an unwanted journey toward an unknown future, we pressed on and continued to put together her playroom. Amidst the appointments, tests, starting her on solid foods in a desperate attempt to stop the reflux, and fears of what was wrong, we continued.

The day of her reflux diagnosis was the day I had already planned to drive to Baltimore with a friend to go shopping at IKEA for her playroom. As she cried and cried—the entire way there and back—and as I pondered the accuracy of the diagnosis, a determination built up inside to finish her playroom.

After the devastating CT scan (that showed "brain abnormalities"), I remember Brennan holding her on the couch in the basement while I labored away to assemble the cubed shelves and the play mat.

I felt increasingly desperate to complete it as each piece of bad news was delivered.

We assembled the IKEA furniture to store her plentiful toys, and we pieced together the colorful floor mat that would provide a more comfortable place for her to play while also teaching her letters, numbers, and colors. I assembled toys and put batteries in when required. I organized and arranged her toys and stuffed animals in colorful Thirty-One bins.

As long as I was working on the room, I felt hopeful: I felt like everything would be okay.

Once her official diagnosis and prognosis were received, I stopped working on her playroom for weeks. I think it was a combination of grief and of learning about feeding tubes and other new medical realities in our lives. The room became a nonpriority.

Once we decided to choose joy and hope, I finished her room. Her playroom represented hope: it demonstrated trust that God still works miracles today and that He could absolutely heal her. I wanted the room to be finished just in case God decided to heal her here on earth. It was an act of faith, in a way.

She still hasn't been able to play with most of her toys or to enjoy her playroom, but lately other children have while their parents visit with us or while we host Bible study meetings for church. I love hearing their laughter and seeing their smiles while they play with Tori's toys.

We continue to pray for her healing with every breath, and we continue to thank God for giving Tori to us, even if just for a little while.

The playroom was intended for joy, and it has brought indeed that, though in a way we never would have expected.

And maybe someday Tori will be playing along with those girls, making a mess (that I long to clean up) and being loud (a sound I would do just about anything to hear). Maybe someday.

Her bedroom used to be my favorite place in our home. It was clean, organized, always clutter-free. It was cheerful, colorful, calming. I made sure it remained perfectly neat at all times, unlike the rest of the house. I would often go in there toward the end of my pregnancy and sit in the glider. I would put my feet up and talk to her, already enjoying our time together in that special space that would soon be hers. We filled her bookshelves with books and her closet with clothes. Friends and family came together to help us get the room ready and to prepare a home for her.

I couldn't wait to make memories in there with her, to read, play, dress up, look at the maps, and enjoy time together.

Once she was here, she and I spent countless hours in that room. That's where I nursed her, rocked her to sleep, played with her, changed her, dressed her. Everything.

Some of my favorite memories of her took place in her room, in her crib.

I discovered at some point that I could lay her down with toys and the mobile running above and I could get things done a few minutes at a time. She would laugh, smile, and play. Many of the best pictures we have of her were taken in those moments.

She loved her changing table, or perhaps simply the undivided attention that she received while on it. She would laugh and smile and move around—we called it dancing. She was pure joy.

And then Krabbe began to take over her body and everything changed.

Night after night we would try to lay her down to sleep in her crib and she refused to sleep. She became inconsolable and we finally brought her into our bed out of desperation.

She would sleep soundly as long as she was near us. Now we know that she longed for the comfort that only parents can give to their baby because she was hurting. Next to us, she felt safe.

And there she still sleeps today.

She has her half of the bed and whoever is the parent on night shift has the other. The other parent sleeps upstairs in order to actually rest and because our queen-size bed is simply not big enough for two adults and a baby on a big pillow.

You do what you have to do.

Slowly, without realizing it, we began using her room less and less until we weren't using it for anything meaningful anymore.

Her room is now used to store medical supplies, clothing, giraffes, and anything else that doesn't have a home amidst the growing number of medical devices taking over our home.

The place that brought so much joy now only brings grief. It is no longer the wonderful, serene place where she and I enjoyed so many hours of loving memories.

It's just a closet.

35 The Beginning of the End

Background Music:
"How Great Is Our God," by Chris Tomlin

Every new beginning comes from some other beginning's end.
—SENECA

In late November 2015, we made our quarterly trip to Pittsburgh for a few days of testing with Dr. Escolar. While we were there, they observed that Tori's oxygen saturation was dipping lower than desired; thus, oxygen concentrators entered the scene. The chest X-ray indicated that she had some atelectasis (a complete or partial collapse of a lung or lobe of a lung, when the tiny air sacs within the lung become deflated) in her lungs, so we were given instructions for additional respiratory therapy routines before heading home. At this point, she was also put on a pulse oximeter around the clock to monitor her oxygen saturation and heart rate. More equipment, more things to monitor.

Despite the new addition of the oxygen, Tori was a bridesmaid in my friend Shannon's wedding on December 5 as part of her bucket list; afterward, Brennan, Tori, and I spent a couple of days at The Hotel Hershey to have a mini-vacation close to home. She slept so well and was so calm—something we took as a blessing and not as an indication that something wasn't right, as we should have.

While at The Hotel Hershey we accomplished some bucket list items and enjoyed our time as a family before heading to Philadelphia for a Flyers game (thanks to one of Tori's supporters, also named Victoria). It was a great week for us and Tori enjoyed the experiences we had. But if there's one thing we learned about our Tori, it was that she went all in when it came to her disease—rarely was anything subtle or gradual.

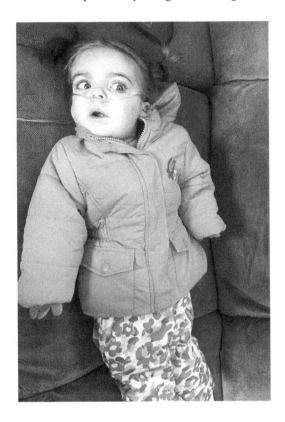

As we headed back to Harrisburg, we noticed that her breathing sounded a bit different; her breaths were shallower and more labored, despite the fact that her oxygen saturation remained good. We decided to take her to the emergency room at Hershey Med that evening and they did a chest X-ray; it showed that she still had some atelectasis, though in a different part of the lungs than the previous X-ray had shown. They recommended that we have her admitted so that they could continue to monitor her and to administer breathing treatments, and we agreed with their decision.

Brennan left the hospital around 10:00 p.m. so that he could rest before work the following morning, and Tori and I waited and waited to be put into a room. It was about midnight by the time we could get settled in a room, and I was so exhausted. Tori remained asleep for most of the night—which was strange and concerning to me, given her hatred of sleep—even during the eleven sticks they did to try to find a vein (all were unsuccessful, likely because they had stopped her feeds just after 6:30 p.m. and she was dehydrated).

I, on the other hand, did not sleep much, as I was awakened constantly by doctors and nurses asking me questions. The most memorable occurrence was around 3:00 a.m. when a doctor in a yellow robe and yellow mask (which they all wore in case Tori had a respiratory infection) woke me up and asked me to walk over with her to look at Tori, who was eight feet away from me. I was confused, but I got up and followed her. Tori was peacefully sleeping and her numbers were great; I told the doctor that I wasn't sure what she wanted from me. The doctor then told me that her sodium level was 114, which is dangerously low.

I immediately became alarmed because it hadn't even been one year since we had last heard the phrase "dangerously low sodium" as the only identifiable cause of death of my friend Shannon's mom, Renee. We were NOT going to lose Tori because of salt!

The doctor told me that the low sodium likely explained Tori's fussiness the week prior, her fatigue (and we thought she had slept well at The Hotel Hershey because it's so luxurious!), and possibly the respiratory issues, as well. While that explanation brought relief because she wasn't sick, it also brought a new level of fear because they couldn't determine why her sodium was so low.

While we were in the hospital, we realized that Tori had been admitted to the hospital almost exactly ten months prior for a feeding tube prediagnosis. That hospital experience was incredibly stressful because we felt like we were in the middle of life or death, waiting for a definitive diagnosis and corresponding treatment—or lack thereof in our case. The time passed so slowly and we never knew how long we would be there. This stay was much different, a relief in many ways.

Caring for Tori at home was challenging and exhausting, sleep deprivation aside. Being in the pediatric intermediate care unit meant there were plenty of people to care for her, including a respiratory therapist every two hours. We knew that she was in the best possible hands.

And yet, despite the relief, we were yet again reminded of her fragility. Of her terminal diagnosis. The first night of our stay, they asked us about life-saving measures, and we had to make decisions about whether to resuscitate or choose DNR, given her prognosis, should that situation arise.

Parents should never have to make these decisions for their children.

I wanted to cuddle with her like we did every day (all day) at home, but she was so attached to monitors that I went nearly two days without holding her. That was thankfully remedied on the third day and I was able to hold her. I slept about eight feet away from her, on the not-so-comfortable hospital couch, and that was the furthest I had slept from her since diagnosis when I was on night duty. It felt so far.

And yet, we were still filled with hope and gratitude each step of the way. We were so blessed to have an amazing children's hospital right in our backyard. She truly was in great hands. We were able to educate so many people about Krabbe during this stay, and that alone is priceless.

We were so touched by the nurses who cared for Tori, as well as other staff members (the man who brought the meals became one of my favorites because of his kind heart and gentle spirit and for how he took care of me). And most of all, we were so thankful to still have Tori in our lives. We knew time was short, and because of this we treasured every moment with her.

Ten months isn't a long time, but so much had changed and we were thankful for our new perspectives.

"As the days float off the calendar I have to remind myself that these days and moments in the hospital count. Just because I'm desperate to get home doesn't mean that a snuggle in the hospital bed means any less. That bath time with disposable washcloths in a tub labeled 4th floor makes the same amount of bubbles and that squeezing a hand with an IV line still gives comfort. Since we started this journey a crack was made in my heart; but we don't live in the crack. We live in the strong part of the heart that knows no limits and serves a miraculous God. So even though we may roll towards

the crack, we will never stay there; we will always make our way
back to the strong part of the heart where we stand together."
—Aᴘʀɪʟ Gᴀʀᴄɪᴀ (Kʀᴀʙʙᴇ ᴍᴏᴍ ᴛᴏ Jᴀᴄᴋꜱᴏɴ)

After a few days, they were content with her sodium levels—which were holding steadily at 139—and we were instructed to continue to add sodium to the breast milk at each meal. They also discontinued one of her medications, as they believed that could have been the culprit. We were happy to be discharged and back at home, where she was the most comfortable and where we could be a family.

While we were in the hospital, Tori's palliative care team asked if we would be interested in having hospice be involved in Tori's care. I was previously under the impression that hospice was only called in when death was imminent, that it was a service used only in a person's last days. So when the idea was presented to us, I was understandably confused. It felt so surreal to be having that discussion, because she was still doing so well. It was then explained to us that a person can be on hospice for years and that it is merely another resource to make our lives easier.

Make things easier? Yes, please.

A few days later, two nurses from Hospice of Central Pennsylvania came over to take care of the "intake" process and to discuss the services they would provide. We were excited about their services—things like medication delivery, nurse visits as needed (including emergency ones before going to the ER in order to keep us home), and anything we might need in the meantime.

Of course, they would also be available to help us with making end-of-life decisions as needed.

That day, I wrote the following:

> End of life. It's still so strange to think that we are
> discussing Tori in these terms. We've heard from others

that hospice was a great blessing during a rough time, so we are glad to have this resource at our disposal.

All of this talk of death has made us, once again, so thankful for the hope of heaven that we have as followers of Jesus. This world is not our home! Scripture tells us that we will be made whole, that we will have no more pain or tears, that our bodies will be whole and restored and made new. We will be living with Jesus and the angels He created (though we do not become angels ourselves) and be reunited with our loved ones who also believed that Jesus is the Son of God. What a family reunion awaits us!

There will be no more death, no more war, no sickness, no conflict. No hunger or thirst. Nothing bad at all. No more Krabbe. What will there be?

Love.

Joy.

Peace.

Patience.

Kindness.

Faithfulness.

Gentleness.

Goodness.

Perfection.

Can you imagine?

The hurt and devastation around the world are overwhelming and only add to my heartbreak, so I try to avoid the news most days. However, the more I read the news, the greater my longing for heaven. I long for the peaceful, perfect place the Bible describes far more now than ever before, and I can't wait to walk with Jesus someday.

Do I want Tori to go to heaven before us? Of course not. We want to keep her with us for the rest of our lives, and we still pray for a miraculous healing. And yet,

if that is God's Will, we know she will be in good hands
until we meet her there someday.

As time passed, we were filled with joy but also with sadness because we were
getting closer to her life expectancy of two years of age or less. We continued
to do bucket list adventures as she was able—one being a photo shoot in my
wedding dress, thanks to Brennan's cousin Sarah Benner. I surprised Brennan
with this adventure and his emotional response made it worth the effort.

Image by Sarah B Photography

Once she reached nineteen months, we could count the expected
number of remaining months on one hand.

And that's when things started to get scary.

February 14, 2016:

We had a scary moment this afternoon—Tori stopped
breathing and turned a shade of blue I have never seen.

Her numbers had been perfect before that moment. I repositioned her, tapped her on the chest, blew on her face, and asked her to breathe with tears welling up in my eyes. She did. Her numbers bounced back from the forties and she was all right again.

In that moment I realized that, even though I know what is going to happen, I will never be prepared to say good-bye.

I was extra scared because I have been praying that she will go when both Brennan and I are with her—not by ourselves. So since he was there, I thought this might be it.

As I got ready for bed, I remembered that scare and tears started to well up in my eyes. I washed my face and I couldn't stop crying. I walked into our bedroom and Brennan could tell I had been crying, and he asked what was wrong. I said, "I just want to be her mom!" And the tears started all over again. He got teary eyed too and said, "And I just want to be her dad." We held each other and cried and talked about how scary it was.

Lately she has had issues pooping, she has been sleeping a lot, and now this. I have a feeling it will be sooner than we want. I want her suffering to be over, but I don't want to say good-bye.

February 15, 2016:

It was my night to sleep, and I was lying down upstairs trying to rest. Suddenly, through the vent, I heard Brennan yelling my name. My heart stopped as I stumbled out of bed, terrified that she was gone.

I ran downstairs and to our bedroom as quickly as I could, panicked. When I got in the room, Brennan was holding Tori up, trying to get her to breathe. Her oxygen

saturation had dropped into the twenties and she was
as blue as I had ever seen her.

Tears streamed down my face as I spoke to her,
frantically trying to persuade her to breathe.

Then she gasped and began breathing heavily and
quickly.

Brennan and I were still shaken for nearly an hour
after that. In that moment we realized that we will
never be prepared for her death. Unlike anything else
in life, preparation will not make the event any easier.

This wouldn't be the last time that her numbers would drop terrifyingly low, unfortunately. That week there were several times that they dropped, the lowest number being thirteen. Thankfully, she bounced back and recovered fairly quickly.

We saw Dr. Escolar the last week of February for Tori's normal quarterly visit. During that visit, she underwent another MRI and it was determined that the disease had progressed to stage four. That didn't mean that death was imminent, as some children remain in stage four for years. Nevertheless, Dr. Escolar advised us to fill out a "Do Not Resuscitate" form so that our wishes would be followed when the time came. It was also noted that her potassium levels were low, so we began adding that to her morning feeds. No one could determine a cause, and since the supplemental potassium seemed to resolve the issue, it wasn't a major concern.

Dr. Escolar squeezed Tori's hand and said, "See you in six months!" instead of our usual three, which meant that she expected Tori to live another six months, that she would live to be at least two years old, and we were filled with a cautious hope once again.

We didn't know it then, but this was the beginning of the end.

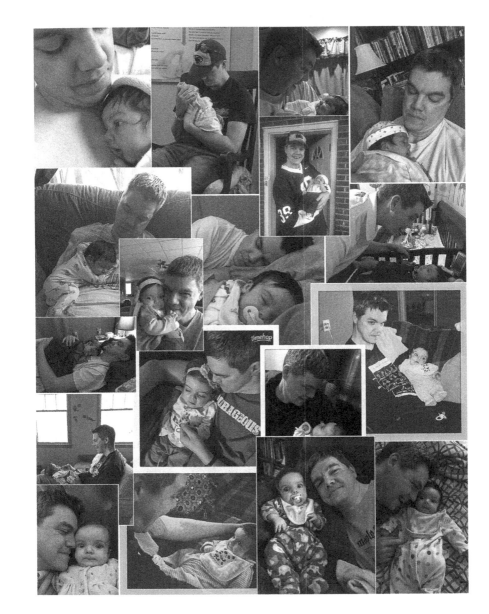

36 A Life Well-Lived

Background Music: "I'd Rather Have Jesus,"
by Alison Krauss & The Cox Family

All of us hope that there is a magnificent purpose for our lives, that there is meaning in our existence. We all want to have an impact on the world and we spend our lives working toward that goal in one way or another, in ways big and small. As parents, we want our children to change the world, to make a tremendous impact on everyone they encounter. We want them to live fulfilling lives that are meaningful.

As Christian parents, we want our children to know and love God and to tell others about His goodness, His love, His sacrifice for us so that they can live with Him in heaven forever. We want our children to experience His love, peace, grace, and mercy, and then show others the same.

As we ponder why God has allowed Tori to have Krabbe, it has become apparent to us that Tori has already made such an impact during her short time on this earth thus far and she hasn't even tried to do so. She has changed perspectives—and even hearts and lives—just by existing. By being such a courageous warrior.

She has changed us in numerous ways, and she has saved the lives of her future siblings (and possibly strangers) in a courageous way. What more could a parent ask for in the life of their child?

If God chooses to heal her here on earth, what a testimony she—and we—will have! God's power and mercy will be evident to all and lives will be changed. But if God chooses to heal her in heaven, we will still have a strong testimony of His grace, His love, His peace, His goodness . . . because we know that He is the only one who can help us get through any of this. Victoria Ruth Brackbill is a world changer, and we can't wait to see how God will continue to use our precious baby, even if it isn't the way we want her story to be written.

We traveled with Tori and had as many adventures as we possibly could in just a few months while she was still doing exceptionally well, but around the same time that the oxygen machine became part of our lives, Tori became less and less happy with going anywhere. She required increased suctioning, she needed to be laid on her side to help with the drooling from teething, and she just seemed to prefer to stay home. I admit that I was reluctant, but Brennan and I realized that we were going to have to drastically alter the way we had been living life. We knew it was time to stay home.

My friend Amy Smoker once spoke about the story of Jacob and Esau, and how Jacob indicated that he needed to travel at the pace of his children because that was best for them. Jacob had been through a great deal in the years leading up to his encounter with Esau. By the time we get to Genesis 33, he has already run in fear from his brother after robbing him of his blessing (Genesis 27), worked for his father-in-law for fourteen years (after being tricked into doing so), wrestled with God (Genesis 32), and now is meeting his brother, Esau, for the first time in decades. He is tired of running, tired of fighting, tired of pushing. Jacob is not the same man he was in Genesis 27, and his response to Esau in Genesis 33:13–14 proves that.

After a tearful and wonderful reconciliation, Esau invites Jacob to travel with him. Jacob says, "You can see, my lord, that some of the children are very young, and the flocks and herds have their young, too. If they are driven too hard, even for one day, all the animals could die. Please, my lord, go ahead of your servant. We will follow slowly, at a pace that is comfortable for the livestock and the children. I will meet you at Seir."

Jacob is no longer pushing; instead, he is traveling at the pace of his children.

Amy wisely used this to challenge all of the mothers in the room by applying this to the comparison game that so many women play, always trying to keep up with our friends in an effort to appear to have the ideal life. She said, "When our approval is from God, we can believe we are exactly the mom our children need. We don't have to keep up with other moms. We can be ourselves as the Lord has made us."

As mothers and fathers, we need to travel at the pace of our children.

Brennan and I took this to heart, and we did just that, even though it required some sacrifices of us—including not going to church between Christmas and Easter because of the possibility of germs entering our home and making Tori sick.

For the first time, we allowed Tori to dictate the pace of our lives, even though it was difficult to stay home from gatherings and activities that we enjoyed. We decided to live life at her pace, which was gradually slowing down and requiring more effort.

> *He takes no pleasure in the strength of a horse or in*
> *human might. No, the Lord's delight is in those who fear*
> *him, those who put their hope in his unfailing love.*
> —PSALM 147:10–11

As time progressed, God gently let me know that Tori wasn't going to be healed on earth. I certainly did not speak this out loud (except to Brennan) or even write it down, but I just knew. So this new way of living—of being at home and slowing down—felt like defeat, like surrender, because we were being forced to accept the truth that our baby girl was going to die, that she was fragile and weak. And there was absolutely nothing we could do to stop it.

37 The California Trip . . . that Wasn't

Background Music:
"Cast My Cares," by Finding Favour

On January 3, 2016, we bought our plane tickets for our next California trip, March 17 to 27. I was nervous about planning that far in advance, because we knew that Tori was nearing her life expectancy with every day that passed. We bought the trip insurance for the first time ever just in case we couldn't go.

Hospice had set us up well with oxygen tanks in Red Bluff—delivered right to my parents' house—and a portable concentrator and extra batteries to get there. The airline required a form to be signed by Tori's doctor to prove that she required oxygen, so we sent it to Dr. Escolar's office the Monday before we were to fly on Thursday.

I followed up with them on Thursday to see if the form had been signed yet and was told that Dr. Escolar was very concerned about Tori flying and wanted to talk to me.

Three and a half hours before we needed to leave for the airport, I received a phone call from Dr. Escolar. She said that Tori could die in flight due to the trauma that the increased pressure from the elevation combined with the extra fluid around her brain (hydrocephalus) would cause, and that she didn't think we should go.

We were devastated. We had added so many new items to Tori's bucket list for this trip—a cable car ride, Fisherman's Wharf, and the Golden Gate Bridge, to name a few. We were going to see so many family members and friends. We knew that this was likely our last trip with her to California, and letting that go was devastating.

But it was devastating to me personally, as well. I needed to go. I needed to see my family and friends. I needed this adventure as a relief from the stress of caring for Tori. Me, me, me. I felt selfish, but I also realized that I had devoted all of my time and energy to Tori's care and it was okay to be disappointed about this trip for "selfish" reasons.

I called Brennan and said, "I know this would be crazy, but let's drive. We're already packed, it would be about forty hours of driving, but we could GO." In a moment of insanity, we decided to go for it. We could arrive by Saturday evening and then leave on Easter morning in order to get back in time for Brennan to return to work.

We loaded up the van and hit the road.

We made it as far as Cleveland that evening when exhaustion took over. We got a hotel room and tried to get some sleep. But I had so much caffeine to get to Cleveland that I couldn't sleep, despite the exhaustion that I felt in every bone. As Brennan and Tori slept, my mind kept racing about the details of the drive before us, and I decided to do some research about our route and what was to come. I discovered that if we drove for sixteen hours the next day, we'd only get as far as Nebraska. That realization made me even more exhausted and I began to question our decision to drive. In addition, there were snow storms headed toward the Rockies, directly in our route.

Thanks to one of my childhood teachers who commented with this information on my Facebook status, I also found out that I-80 goes as high as 8,900 feet in Wyoming. Elevation. Tori's brain.

At 5:30 a.m., I woke Brennan up and told him all that I had been considering and we decided that the wisest decision would be to turn around and go home. We were disappointed, but we recognized that it just wasn't wise to try to drive across the country for so many reasons.

My parents decided to use their tax refund to fly out to Pennsylvania to see us. In an effort to revive our desire for adventure and to ease our disappointment, my parents suggested that we rent an RV (knowing that Tori traveled well in the RV in Arizona in October) and take a road trip around New England. My dad needed eight more states—mostly in New England—to complete his collection (we all hope to visit all fifty states, and it's quite the competition in our family). We agreed and made all the arrangements.

This trip would also ensure that Tori was out of the house while the wall in our living room / kitchen was being removed—a project that we had started in order to make our home more accessible for her and her equipment to more easily maneuver around the first floor. The dust would certainly be harmful to her delicate lungs, so this was a perfect solution.

> *Our hearts ache, but we always have joy.*
> —2 CORINTHIANS 6:10

My parents arrived in Pennsylvania on Monday evening and we left for New England on Tuesday afternoon. Tori's total went up to fifteen states and my dad got his fiftieth. We went through Delaware, New Jersey, New York, and Connecticut before stopping at our cousin's house for the evening. The next day we went through Rhode Island, Massachusetts, New Hampshire (drove the entire coast line—all eighteen miles), Maine, and Vermont. The entire trip felt rushed—God was pushing us home, but we didn't see it then. Ice and snow were forecasted; no RV parks were open. We didn't have many options so we headed to upstate New York.

Tori was comfortable during all of the traveling; she slept a great deal and only had a few blue episodes, so we were thankful that she, yet again, seemed to love traveling and having adventures.

We made it to my Aunt Becky and Uncle Patrick's house in upstate New York that evening and spent two full days with them. While there, we decided to do two of Tori's bucket list items—jumping in a puddle and an Easter egg hunt. Both adventures were a great success, but the Easter egg hunt was my personal favorite. Tori always loved to be outside, and this was no exception. That Friday afternoon was the perfect time to do this with her, and she was awake, alert, and taking everything in. Everyone participated with her and we had a great time as a family, watching Tori's beautiful eyes looking for those colorful eggs.

Throughout our trip everyone took turns cuddling with her and loving her, and I used that opportunity to try out my new camera; I was able to capture beautiful images of my parents, aunt, and uncle holding Tori, as well as great photos of her bucket list adventures.

It was a perfect ending to her short time on earth.

38 "From Life's First Cry to Final Breath..."

Background Music:
"In Christ Alone," by Adie Camp and Geoff Moore

We returned from our New England road trip on Saturday afternoon and began unpacking and settling in again. It was my mom's birthday and she wanted to go to dinner at a local favorite, so Brennan offered to stay home with Tori while my parents and I went to dinner. I welcomed the break and the opportunity to spend time with my parents without interruptions.

When we got back late that evening, Brennan said that Tori had been great and her numbers were excellent. My dad asked to hold her, so Brennan and I began to transfer her into his arms. Once she was lying comfortably in his arms, her numbers started to drop and she had another "blue episode"—this time the oxygen saturation dropped to 4 percent, which was the lowest it had ever been. We quickly moved her back to her pillow and desperately asked her to breathe, while reminding ourselves to do the same. During these episodes, her chest would rise as if she were breathing but no air was entering or exiting her lungs, and it was terrifying.

As always, she bounced back and seemed to be fine again, so we went to bed. It was Brennan's turn for the night shift, so I went upstairs in hopes of getting some good sleep. I told Brennan, as always, to text or call if he needed anything. He had never done so, but I reminded him anyway.

My phone rang at 5:01 a.m. and it was Brennan.

As I struggled to wake up, I was trying to comprehend why he was calling. I quickly realized that something must be wrong with Tori. I ran downstairs to find him holding her; her pulse ox was flatlined and beeping, and she was blue.

She was gone. We used our stethoscope to try to find a heartbeat, but there was none.

Time of death: 5:01 a.m.

We were not entirely unsurprised, given that we had lived with this diagnosis for fourteen months, but it was still a shock. Just two days before she was so alert and was hunting Easter eggs. Now she was in the arms of Jesus. In retrospect, her blue episodes were an indication that her time on earth was short, but we didn't know it at the time.

We both were sobbing and weeping, feeling in that moment a way that words can't accurately describe. I didn't get to say good-bye. I wasn't there. My biggest fear had come true, and I was broken. My only prayer had been that all three of us would be together when she went to heaven, and God seemingly ignored that prayer. I was devastated.

My parents (who were in the basement) heard us crying and came upstairs. My dad took Tori and held her so we could make calls; he held her skin to skin and she was definitely not breathing. No pulse. A limp, lifeless rag doll.

Brennan called hospice and they said it would be about an hour before they could arrive. We continued to notify family, despite the very early hour on both coasts.

My dad held his precious granddaughter tightly, in shock that she was gone.

My parents remained in our bedroom with Tori while Brennan and I were in the kitchen, struggling to grasp that the moment we had dreaded for fourteen months was upon us.

And then, my parents heard a sigh.

None of us had any idea what happens when someone has passed away, so they thought that perhaps this was just part of the process. Then, a deep breath followed by silence. And then another, even closer to the last. Tori's eyes popped open wide and my mom yelled, "Lesa! She's alive!" Brennan and I ran into the room and we all stared in amazement and wonder, having no idea what was going on. We hooked up her pulse ox again and rejoiced that she was alive!

Time of awakening: 5:15 a.m.

The oxygen concentrator roared to life again and we put the cannula back into her nose. We cried and held her and praised God for this chance to say good-bye, if that is what needed to happen. A glimmer of hope appeared in our hearts that her coming back to life was a sign of complete healing. All we could do was wait at this point.

The hospice nurse came out and assessed her and said she seemed to be doing great. Her numbers were perfect—better than they had been in weeks—and she was comfortable. We were hopeful that maybe she would bounce back and that we would have her for a few more months. The nurse stayed for about an hour and eventually asked if we were okay with her leaving since Tori was doing so well.

I took a few pictures of her with my camera and my phone while she was resting, just in case it was my last opportunity, as we had already decided that no pictures would be taken of her once she had gone to heaven. Brennan's mom and sister, Kelly, came by and stayed with us for a little while, holding Tori and talking to her.

Brennan and I put her in the middle of our bed on her pillow and cuddled with her. We didn't know if this was it, or if she'd continue to defy the odds. We hoped desperately that God had fully healed her during those fourteen minutes of death and that He had brought her back to life restored and renewed. We lay down around 7:45 a.m. and all fell asleep, together, me holding Tori's hand and Brennan's hand on her back.

At 9:01 a.m. the pulse ox beeped and I woke up to suction Tori to clear her airway, much as I had done continually over the past nine months. But her numbers continued to drop.

And she didn't take another breath.

I woke Brennan up and we told her we loved her, and through tears, I said that if she wanted to go to Jesus, it was okay.

The pulse ox continued to drop until it finally flatlined, and we turned it off for the last time. We shut down the oxygen concentrator, and our home was once again filled with silence.

Time of death: 9:05 a.m.

We called hospice and Brennan's parents again and held our baby girl's lifeless body close. She was like a rag doll, and it was evident that she was completely gone again—forever this time. Our precious daughter who had just done an Easter egg hunt two days prior was now in the arms of Jesus, healed and whole on the very day He rose again two thousand years ago.

Tori's story began on Easter Sunday 2009 when Brennan and I met, and her earthly journey ended on Easter Sunday 2016 when she entered the gates of heaven, healed and whole.

Once hospice arrived, they began making the necessary phone calls to the mortuary and the oxygen/equipment suppliers for us. We began going through the contacts on our phones and calling some, but mostly copying and pasting the same text: "Sorry to say this through text, but we lost Tori at 9:05 a.m. She is with Jesus now!"

I kept saying, "This is the weirdest day of my life" as I went through the motions of everything that had to be done. And it was. We knew our daughter was dying for fourteen months. We knew that. But we never knew exactly how it would happen. We had so much "unknown" in the midst of the known, and that was unsettling.

Yet the tears didn't flow as I had always expected after she was truly gone the second time. Instead, I was overcome by peace, joy, relief. I had been able to tell her many more times that I love her, that it was okay to go to Jesus. I was able to say good-bye. God had answered my prayer after all, in a far more powerful way than I could have imagined.

As Brennan tried desperately to call me while also trying to get Tori to breathe again, he accidentally left me a voice mail. I made the mistake of listening to it the day after Tori went to heaven, because I was curious to know what it was. That voice mail haunts me to this day. He had called me a few times that morning but would throw the phone on the bed when I didn't answer to be able to care for Tori. He didn't mean to leave a voice mail, but it happened.

On it, I could hear the constant beeping of the pulse-ox, which meant that her heart had stopped beating; I could hear the suction machine as Brennan desperately tried to clear her airway in hopes that she would breathe again; but what haunts me the most is hearing my beloved husband's broken voice saying one word: "Tori." The hopelessness and pain in his voice was palpable and desperate, and I can still hear it. I deleted that voice mail after listening to it, because I couldn't bear to have it on my phone any longer. To this day, I still can't explain why it bothered me enough to delete it, but no matter how hard I try, I cannot delete it from my memory.

Long before Tori went to heaven, we had been advised by many to make certain decisions as soon as possible so that when the time came we were prepared. I am so thankful for that wise advice because it made Easter morning go smoothly despite all that had to be done.

Brennan and I had decided that it was important to donate Tori's brain and spinal cord to research in an effort to help cure or even eradicate this disease, so Dr. Escolar—who was also surprised by Tori's death that day—helped us set all of that into motion. The autopsy was done the next day and the hospital called us before and after the procedure, so that we would know when it was finished.

While Tori was still alive, it had felt so strange and even wrong to think about donating her brain. I couldn't handle the idea most days, even though I knew that it would help save lives and that she wouldn't be in her body any longer. Because of that, I was surprised at how easy it became to discuss the donation with the pathologists and all those who called. The decision to donate became simple and meaningful. We could have chosen to leave her body intact, but what good would that have done for research? The brain would have deteriorated in the ground, never helping anyone else. We knew we had to donate her nervous system in hopes that they would help find a cure for this horrible disease.

We were thankful that a foundation, Partners for Krabbe Research, covered the expenses associated with the autopsy and donation—because health insurance stops once your heart does. Yet another blessing in the midst of pain.

The funeral home asked us when we would want them to come get Tori's body, and we told them to come around 11:30 a.m. That gave us all the opportunity to hold her, to change her diaper and her clothes, brush her hair and put it back into pigtails, and say good-bye.

When she began to get cold, we wrapped her body in a blanket for our own comfort, because at that point it began to be weird. Bodies shouldn't be that cold. Skin shouldn't look so gray. We continued to cuddle with her until it was finally time to take our final moments with her body (I continue to say "her body" because we know she isn't in it any longer. Her soul is with Jesus and all that is left is her flesh and bones, her earthly vessel).

As we cuddled together, Brennan played the song that for most of Tori's life had brought her solace when she was fussy—"Greater" by MercyMe—knowing that when the music stopped, it would be time to let her go forever.

The woman (Catelyn) from the funeral home was so gentle and gracious. She gave very clear instructions and laid blankets on the couch. She told me to lay Tori's body on the blankets and to wrap them around her. When we pulled the blanket over Tori's head, it felt so real. You don't put a blanket over a living baby's head.

Catelyn gently picked up Tori's body, and Brennan and I followed her to the vehicle. It wasn't a hearse, thankfully—it was a minivan much like ours, and it wasn't scary. We watched as Tori's body was laid onto a bed-like structure in the back of the van and Catelyn closed the door.

As Brennan and I walked back to the house, it felt so strange. We had just said our final farewell to our daughter's broken, lifeless body. The moment we had dreaded for over a year had finally happened.

At that point, I decided to take a shower, mostly as an introvert escape from people who were in our home. It felt so good to just be alone, to take a long shower for the first time in a while, to just "be" on this very weird day.

Relief flooded my soul, and I felt almost guilty about that. However, I reminded myself that no one else besides Brennan and me could possibly understand how much we had grieved since diagnosis day. No one else could even begin to imagine how stressful my life had been in the past couple of months as her "blue episodes" increased and her care became more intense. No one could relate to the panic that accompanied each and every one of those episodes as I wondered every time if this was it, if she was going to leave us right then.

It is okay for me to feel relieved for both her and for us. Relief doesn't mean that I didn't love her, or that I wouldn't have continued to care for her as long as she wanted to fight. Relief for me meant that I was rejoicing that she wasn't struggling to breathe anymore. She wasn't suffering. She wasn't broken any longer. I only wanted what was best for her, and on February 13, 2015, we realized that if God wasn't going to heal her here on earth, then heaven was truly best for our Tori because Krabbe was going to rob her of every ability. Heaven, of course, means that we are separated for a little while, but in light of eternity that separation is a mere vapor. We'll see her soon.

39 Pondering Normal and Reveling in the Known

Background Music:
"I Have This Hope," by Tenth Avenue North

Everyone grieves differently. Every situation is unique and every person in every situation handles things differently. I have never been a very emotional person—it's just not how I am wired. I cried more between diagnosis day and the day of Tori's death than in my entire life combined, I'm sure. There were so many days that I would get tears in my eyes while holding her, because my love for her was so fierce and so strong and the thought of losing her was unbearable. We truly grieved in reverse—beginning the day we heard the word Krabbe.

Diagnosis day I was in a fog, unable to function, crying so many tears. I expected to react to her heaven-going similarly, but it didn't happen that way. That is partly because we see God's hand in every single aspect of how, where, and when she died.

I realized recently that part of our inner joy and peace comes from the knowledge that we don't have to wonder anymore when she will be taken from us. We don't have to live each day wondering if it will be her last.

In retrospect, we can see that Tori's brain had been struggling for about six weeks before she went to heaven. Though we rarely spoke of this outside our home or on social media, she had been having "blue episodes" every few days, and the first few scared us so much. We were so panicked when they happened, as we watched her oxygen saturation drop as low as 10 percent at times.

She always jumped right back up to the high nineties, though, and she was alert and responsive even during these episodes, so we weren't concerned about losing her soon. Dr. Escolar was aware of these and acknowledged that Tori was in stage four, but she wanted our next appointment to be in six months as opposed to our usual quarterly visits. She wasn't concerned about losing her soon.

Yet every time one of these episodes happened, our hearts filled with fear and dread as we wondered if this was it. Would she leave us now? Tomorrow? Months from now? We had no idea.

The unknown took its toll on our hearts and minds, even as we tried desperately to trust the Lord and His plan in those moments.

We shed many tears during those blue episodes because they reminded us of her fragility.

One month before she passed away, we had blogged about feeling unprepared to lose her. We couldn't even begin to imagine how we would handle it.

Now we are amazed at how well God actually did prepare us without us even realizing it—every blue episode, every new piece of equipment, all of this worked to remind our hearts that she wouldn't be with us much longer. This knowledge that God was faithful—along with the knowledge that she is whole and healed and with Jesus—has brought us abundant joy and peace.

Though it feels strange to say this, one of my favorite lines that I have written on our blog is this:

> The joy doesn't replace the heartache; rather, they tensely coexist each day, fighting for our undivided attention.

This is true today, as well. It's tempting to have regrets, to wonder what we could have done differently, but the Lord gently reminds our hearts that our number of days are written in His book before we are born; so we shouldn't feel guilty about what we could have done. It would have made no difference.

Even in the wake of Tori's death, joy wins. Peace wins. God wins.

We had previously planned to have Easter dinner at our home with my parents; Brennan's mom, Amy; his sister, Kelly; and her husband, Angel. My sister, Cheyenne, arrived to be with us also, and we went ahead and ate together, and the laughter began as we talked about life and, of course, Tori.

I'm not sure how most people spend their day after their child dies, but we aren't most people, and that's not a new realization. We know that we are unique.

We had ordered a new bed frame the week prior because ours had cracked and wasn't repairable. So that afternoon I asked my dad and Brennan if they wanted to put it together, and they agreed. We cleaned our room (I admit, for the first time in months) and rearranged the furniture in an effort to create a fresh, new space just in case it would bother us that Tori had died in our room.

Then my mom, Cheyenne, and I went shopping to buy new curtains and a new comforter—both of which had been needed for a long while but which we hadn't had a chance to purchase. I asked my mom and Cheyenne while we were shopping if it was weird that we were at Walmart the day that our daughter had died . . . because it seemed like this wasn't what we "should" be doing.

But then I noted that we were simply living out the words we had used throughout Tori's life. Us doing normal things didn't mean that we didn't miss her or that we were glad she wasn't with us—it simply meant that we recognized that she was with Jesus and that we had work to do while we were still on earth.

♡

We will always love our girl, and we will never be the same. But how can we not praise the One who made her, who so perfectly orchestrated her entire life and even her death?

As God said to Job and to Isaiah thousands of years ago, *who are we to question Him?* Who are we to challenge the One who knows everything and created it all?

Just as He knows each star by name and each hair on our heads, so He also knows exactly why all of this happened and how it will unfold. We take joy in knowing that this same God loves us and will never leave us.

Krabbe needs to be known. Every baby deserves to be tested for this wretched disease at birth so that they have a chance at life. Ignorance is NOT bliss when it comes to leukodystrophies, and we will continue to educate people so that no one else has to go through what we have gone through.

Our hearts ache to hold our beautiful daughter once more, but in the meantime, we will continue to advocate and fight in her honor to eradicate this disease from the face of the earth. It's the least we can do.

40 The Morning After

Background Music:
"Hallelujah," by Heather Williams

I was the first one awake the morning after Tori went to heaven, and I was immediately aware of the silence. I wrote this as I pondered our new reality:

> For the past four months we have had the constant humming of an oxygen concentrator in our home. Every few minutes we would hear the loud noise of the suction machine. There was constant noise and we eventually became numb to it all . . . until it stopped.
>
> We turned off the oxygen concentrator when Tori went to heaven and were immediately aware of the loud silence that filled our home. When I woke up this morning, our home was completely silent. As it has been said before, silence is deafening. It is difficult, because those machines helped keep Tori comfortable and reminded us that she was still alive.
>
> But more than anything, the silence is comforting. It means that our Tori is no longer reliant on supplemental oxygen, suction machines, and other devices. She is KRABBE-FREE. Her body is no longer being ravaged by this horrific disease.
>
> As Brennan has said many times, we are inherently selfish humans, so we never wanted to let her go. Yet as parents, the most selfless thing we could do was allow

her to go to heaven as she did, where we KNOW we will see her again someday soon and spend eternity with her.

When Tori left us on Sunday, she couldn't smile, talk, move, laugh, yawn, or even sneeze. She needed oxygen to function. She was broken.

Our hearts are so overwhelmed with joy at the knowledge that she can do ALL of these things and even more now that she is with Jesus.

Yesterday her brain and spinal cord were donated to the University of Pittsburgh to further their research of Krabbe. Today we will take this dress and (a duplicate of) her giraffe buddy to the funeral home for them to dress her for the last time. We have chosen to not see her body again on this earth, because she isn't in it.

Our lives will never be the same, but we will continue to live as we did while Tori was with us—with purpose, with love, and with JOY. We taught her to live with joy and love despite our circumstances, and we need to continue to live that way until we meet her again. It won't be that long in the grand scheme of eternity.

Tori has been in heaven for twenty-six hours now, and while we miss her deeply, I cannot express the peace that I feel.

I have often pondered over the past fourteen months whether it is "better" (as if there is any good way) to lose a child suddenly or over time.

To lose one suddenly and unexpectedly means that they usually don't suffer and it is quick, but you don't always get to say good-bye. To lose one over time, as we did, means that you watch them deteriorate and you grieve for an undetermined period of time. But you can cherish each moment and make purposeful memories with them, grieving along the way. I now know that the way we lost Tori is the "better" way.

We have no regrets about how we lived out her

life. We knew we only had her for a short time on this earth, and we treasured every moment.

Yes, we loved our adventures with her and loved checking off bucket list items: but what we loved most of all was that we spent hundreds—maybe thousands— of hours holding her, cuddling with her, loving her. It was our favorite thing to do.

We chose joy—and continue to do so—and when she left this earth yesterday, we were somewhat ready. (Is any parent ever fully ready? No.) We feel immense peace that is from the Lord alone.

We will likely go through the grieving process again, but I think it will be a little easier this time (as opposed to the past fourteen months of our lives) because we know she is healed. She is happy. She is in the best possible place and is with Jesus.

We cannot express how stressful the past few months have been at times, as caring for her became increasingly intense and she began having "episodes" of turning slightly blue on occasion. Overall she was doing well still, but there were moments of panic in the last month.

It is going to take months to recover from the level of stress we have lived on.

We thought Tori was going to live longer, but we are so thankful that she didn't suffer. She was never sick! She never had seizures. She was only hospitalized one time postdiagnosis. She was so fortunate in so many ways and we know that God protected her.

God is great, faithful, gracious, and loving. We trust His plan and can't wait to see how He continues to use Tori. We are so thankful that God gave Victoria to us and we know that she will continue to change lives.

She had so many adventures in her almost twenty months of life. She brought so much joy to so many.

And most importantly, her life will save lives! We will never stop fighting for newborn screening for ALL babies.

She is healed! She doesn't need oxygen any longer, she doesn't struggle to swallow, and she isn't in pain.

Because of our faith in Jesus and what He did this Easter weekend 2,000 years ago, we have the hope that we will only be separated from her for a short while. We will one day be reunited with her in eternity and she will be WHOLE. She will be able to run around and talk and smile again.

We love our Tori and miss her more than our words can express. But we are so thankful that we are assured of where she is and that she is HEALED.

That same morning, the oxygen supply company called and asked if they could come pick up the portable concentrator we had rented for our trip. Since hospice had called them the day before, I assumed that they knew that she had died; so I asked the man I was speaking with if he would be picking up everything else at the same time.

There was silence on the other end of the line, and after a few moments he asked, "Has Tori been discharged from oxygen?" It was my turn to pause, and then I responded with "Yes, yes she has." She had been discharged by the Great Physician and was breathing freely! I then informed him that she had passed away the day prior, so we no longer needed the oxygen in our home.

While some Krabbe families had relayed that it was difficult to see their child's equipment taken away, I couldn't get it out of our home soon enough. It was bulky and took up so much space throughout our house, and it was a constant reminder that she was fragile, that she was dying. After the oxygen equipment was removed, I immediately called the respiratory supply company to have them come pick up all of their equipment—the suction machines, the cough assist, the pulse oximeter, the nebulizer. As grateful as we were to have those machines to help Tori breathe more freely and to prevent aspiration, I was even more grateful to see them leave our house forever.

In a way, I resented the respiratory care equipment. I used it faithfully to care for Tori, but every fiber of my being resisted it because I didn't want her to need it. I didn't want her to be reliant on the suction machine because she couldn't swallow, or the oxygen concentrator because she couldn't breathe. I didn't want any of this. But now she was free, free from Krabbe, from equipment, from this life that was never really hers. Free.

41 Abundant Gratefulness

Background Music:
"Amazing Grace" (hymn)

Don't worry about anything; instead, pray about everything.
Tell God what you need, and thank him for all he has done.
Then you will experience God's peace,
which exceeds anything we can understand.
His peace will guard your hearts and minds as you live in Christ Jesus.
—Philippians 4:6–7

Always be joyful. Never stop praying.
Be thankful in all circumstances,
for this is God's will for you who belong to Christ Jesus.
—1 Thessalonians 5:16–18

We have been overwhelmed by God's faithfulness and His grace in all of the events surrounding Tori's home going—which are nothing short of miraculous. It's been stunning, really, even though we shouldn't be surprised. He is a great God who loves His children. I'm not sure I ever expected to describe a death as miraculous, but it truly was. God's hand was so evidently working to make things happen the way they did!

Brennan and I had many specific prayers about Tori's passing that we had been praying for months, and God answered our prayers in many ways. Here are the things we noticed, but I'm sure there are even more that will become evident as time progresses:

- We were home, not in California, and we were together.
- We bought trip insurance for the first time ever, ensuring that we would get our money back from our cancelled flights to and from California, which made it easier to choose to stay home.
- Tori came back to say good-bye and to give us peace with her second passing.
- She went peacefully, in her sleep.
- We didn't have to invoke the DNR and make the choice to let her pass. God did it.
- My parents were here and not in California.
- We spent the prior week traveling together—something we all love—and were able to create new memories with her.
- Brennan was with Tori constantly for nine full days before she passed.
- We never had to adjust to home nursing, which would have been a mixed blessing.
- I took many photos of her during her last days of life on earth because I was so excited about my new camera.
- She never knew sickness—not even a cold.
- She never greatly suffered.
- She wasn't in extreme pain thanks to her medicines, and therefore didn't have to be on any intense medications like morphine or Valium—only a low dose of gabapentin.
- She was only hospitalized once postdiagnosis, and that was to stabilize sodium, nothing intrusive.
- God chose Brennan and me to be Tori's parents. What an amazing, humbling honor. He could have given her to anyone, but He chose us. We are so thankful for that.

The root of joy is gratefulness. It is not joy that makes
us grateful, it is gratitude that makes us joyful.
—DAVID STEINDL-RAST

Our gratitude also includes the work of the Holy Spirit in both our lives and the lives of others. Friends shared the following stories with us, indicating that the Holy Spirit was at work at the time Tori passed:

> I wanted to write you a quick message as something quite unexpected happened yesterday. As I was sitting in church (before hearing the news) I was praying for Tori . . . and suddenly had a glimpse of her as a resurrected self. In that moment, I sat in awe of Christ's hope, but had no idea how present it was.
>
> Our church starts at 9:00 a.m. and this past Sunday it started a little late. Our daughter, who never talks about Tori but has known the whole story since she was diagnosed, saw Tori's name on our prayer list, where it has been for over a year. She said, "It's so nice that we pray for Tori. Don't worry: she will be okay, Mommy." After church, as we headed to my parents', I received the text of Tori's departure.

I never expected to be grateful for aches and pains, but one seems to be straight from the Lord. After Tori went to heaven, I realized that the tendinitis I developed suddenly about two months before Tori's death served a greater purpose than I realized. I developed this condition in my left arm from sitting and holding her for many hours each day. It got so bad that I could barely grab a water bottle, and my arm was so weak that it was difficult to hold her head up. Because of this, I was forced to lay her on her pillow more frequently to alleviate the pain. In the final two months of her precious life, I gradually held her less and less.

I truly believe God was preparing me to never hold her again.

> *For these things—and more—we are so thankful. We cannot help but praise the One who made her, the One who so evidently put all of this into place in His perfect timing. His Word is yet again proving to be true: "The joy of the Lord is your strength!"* (Nehemiah 8:10)

I have long been taught that gratitude is the antidote to anger, jealousy, bitterness, and other such attitudes. The week after Tori went to heaven, I learned that gratitude can also lessen the blow of deep sorrow. We will—and do—have moments of sorrow as we miss her presence here with us, but we stand in awe of our loving and gracious God who so perfectly arranged so many details so that we could find peace in Tori's passing.

> *You saw me before I was born.*
> *Every day of my life was recorded in your book.*
> *Every moment was laid out*
> *before a single day had passed.*
> (Psalm 139:16)

God is good, faithful, loving, and gracious. That has never changed and never will

A few days after Tori went home, I remembered the wise words my dear friend Heatherly Walker had shared three months prior:

One of the passages of Scripture I have pondered since Tori was diagnosed was 2 Samuel 12, where David is told that his baby would die. My husband preached a few days ago about David begging, pleading, fasting, and praying for the life of his child. And God said no. This is where we see the David-being-a-man-after-Gods-heart thing in action. David gets up, washes, dresses, eats, and then goes to worship God.

I get so angry about the small things. My trust falters. My fist has shaken toward the heavens. And here is a father, who has lost his child, praising God not in exchange for a miracle. But just because of who He is and is worthy of our praise.

I know you have your moments. But I see this heart of worship being built in you.

After the loss, David was given Solomon. The world is still impacted over these two babies.

Here is the scripture passage:

> David begged God to spare the child. He went without food and lay all night on the bare ground. The elders of his household pleaded with him to get up and eat with them, but he refused.
>
> Then on the seventh day the child died. David's advisers were afraid to tell him. "He wouldn't listen to reason while the child was ill," they said. "What drastic thing will he do when we tell him the child is dead?"
>
> When David saw them whispering, he realized what had happened. "Is the child dead?" he asked.

> *"Yes," they replied, "he is dead."*
>
> *Then David got up from the ground, washed himself, put on lotions, and changed his clothes. He went to the Tabernacle and worshiped the LORD. After that, he returned to the palace and was served food and ate.*
>
> *His advisers were amazed. "We don't understand you," they told him. "While the child was still living, you wept and refused to eat. But now that the child is dead, you have stopped your mourning and are eating again."*
>
> *David replied, "I fasted and wept while the child was alive, for I said, 'Perhaps the LORD will be gracious to me and let the child live.' But why should I fast when he is dead? Can I bring him back again? I will go to him one day, but he cannot return to me." (2 Samuel 12:16–23)*

What I hadn't considered until this friend mentioned it was this: the story didn't end there. After David lost his son, he was blessed with another son—Solomon, the wisest man who ever lived.

David's greatest legacy was still to come.

> *Then David comforted Bathsheba, his wife, and slept with her. She became pregnant and gave birth to a son, and David named him Solomon. (2 Samuel 12:24)*

After we were reminded of her message to us, Brennan and I discussed how strange it was that we didn't feel the deep sorrow we imagined that we would after losing Tori. We realize that grief is a process, but we truly believe that we grieved deeply over the fourteen months after her diagnosis while we had the knowledge that she would leave us far too soon.

Her final breath brought us closure. It brought us peace.

I realized that—without even trying to do so—like David, we had risen from our knees and were praising God for all He had done. It wasn't an intentional or conscious action (and we certainly aren't spiritual superheroes or anything like that)—we were simply overcome by His undeniable presence and the incredible workings of His hands to orchestrate Tori's miraculous death. We couldn't help but praise Him as we marveled at all of the details and the amazing things He had done.

Like David, we pleaded and begged for Tori's life to be spared, for us to be able to enjoy our precious daughter on earth for the rest of our lives. We begged Him for fourteen months and waited for His final answer.

The Lord gently said no that Sunday and our hearts are at peace. A peace only He can give. We trust His Word, and we trust that He has something incredible in store for our lives, and that Tori's short life was just the beginning. The impact of her life on the world is not fully known, and we can't wait to see how it unfolds. In the meantime, we will continue to praise Jesus for the things He has done and all He has yet to do.

42 Tori's Celebration of Life

Background Music:
"Home," by Chris Tomlin

*It may not be well with your circumstances,
but it can be well with your soul.*
—TAMMY TRENT

As we drove home from Maryland after attending the memorial of another Krabbe baby—Parker Shoemaker—in September 2015, we discussed the need to begin to think about what we wanted to do after Tori passed away. We didn't know what state of mind we would be in after the inevitable happened, so we determined that it would be best to have everything written out; and if it wasn't needed because God healed her, all the better!

We began to think through the obvious decisions: burial or cremation (the thought of cremating her was too much for either of us to handle, so we decide that burial was the only way, but the location remained a question), whether or not to donate her brain / spinal cord to research, and so forth. Where would we bury her if we chose that option? Since we weren't certain about where we would "put down roots," we didn't know where (or even in which state) we should bury her earthly body. Would it bother us to move away and leave her body in Pennsylvania? It was impossible to determine these things in the moment, so we continued to think about them for a few weeks.

One day as I was pondering these things, I had the idea to bury her body at the Hershey Cemetery. When Brennan came home from work, I told him my idea, prefacing it with, "I know this sounds crazy, but . . ." because to anyone else, it would likely sound strange. Thankfully, he agreed wholeheartedly and thought it was the perfect location and reason. Mr. and Mrs. Hershey are also buried in the Hershey Cemetery, and given the love and respect we have for them, and knowing how much they loved children, it brought us peace knowing that Tori would be there with them, even though we knew rationally that no one is actually there—it's only their earthly remains. When you're in a situation like ours, though, you take whatever brings you peace.

We also decided early on that we just wanted a wooden box for her burial. A simple wooden box. We contacted our friend, Dean Byler, about constructing it for us, and he was honored by our request. He spent three days after Tori passed away building a beautiful box complete with a family of giraffes that he burned into the top. It far exceeded any expectations we had—it was truly too beautiful to bury six feet under the ground. The level of detail was stunning, and we were so thankful for his craftsmanship.

As we thought about the memorial service aspect of all of this, we knew that it needed to be a giant party—a true celebration of life. No black. No mourning. Just joyful memories. We'd have balloons and other bright and fun things. And, of course, Tori's entire giraffe collection would be in attendance—all 150-plus giraffes that had been sent to her from all over the world.

We felt content with what we decided, though we hoped we would never need that list. So when Tori went to heaven, we were prepared, practically speaking. Plans were set in motion and we had plenty of friends and family members to assist.

We chose to have a private burial on the Friday after Easter, and planned for her celebration of life to be held nearly two weeks after her passing to allow for traveling.

As we searched for a suitable location that would hold hundreds of people, The Hotel Hershey (Brennan's place of employment since 2003) offered us the largest room they had available for that Saturday; we gladly accepted the offer, even though we knew it only held 250 people. The hotel has great meaning to us, and Tori spent quite a bit of time there, so it was fitting.

We put up an official "invite" on Facebook and watched as the RSVP numbers climbed rapidly. By the next morning, over 300 people said they were coming and another 100 said "maybe." We realized that we were going to have to find another location, and it would have to be fast!

After dozens of phone calls to and messages left for nearly every hotel, conference center, museum, and large church in our area, we received just one phone call back: LCBC—a large church not far from us—was willing and able to accommodate our request! As it turns out, the pastors had been following Tori's story from the beginning and were thrilled to be able to serve our family in this way.

The location couldn't have been any more perfect. The large lobby area was ideal for setting up all of Tori's six Project Life photo albums (which I had meticulously compiled throughout her life instead of scrapbooks), hanging the canvas pictures of her on the walls, displaying the slideshow on a TV, allowing for space for the kids to color giraffe coloring pages (thanks to our friend Wendy Kerstetter), and, of course, room for some of her giraffes. My dad had the idea to line the stage with her giraffes, and seeing them all up there was impressive. We have no idea how all 150 fit in her room! All shapes and sizes and colors, from all over the world. The giraffe is forever going to remind people of our Tori.

Brennan and I had decided months beforehand that worship was going to be one of the primary components of her celebration, so I assembled what I called my "worship dream team" of some of the musicians with whom I had led worship in Pennsylvania over the past fourteen years. The team was composed of Becky Saxe (my aunt) and Dean Byler on keyboards and vocals, Tom Ritter on electric guitar, Tommy Toone on drums, and me, leading the way vocally. It was just another way we displayed that we were choosing to celebrate, not mourn.

After my dad welcomed everyone, Brennan took the stage and spoke from his heart about Tori. He encouraged everyone to live life well: *"We lived a lot of life in a short amount of time with Tori. . .As we plug along in life we have dreams and aspirations. . .and then life gets in the way. Instead of letting life get in the way, why don't we get in the way of life? We aren't promised tomorrow, so live life today."*

Following Brennan was his best friend, Pastor Jeremy Kerstetter, who spoke and did an incredible job of pointing everyone to the God we serve in addition to highlighting the life that Tori lived. Using photography as a metaphor, Jeremy pointed out that we often let the world control our focus instead of controlling it ourselves. *"As we look at Tori's life, we can see that God has used her to adjust our focus on life . . . On Easter morning she was freed from her earthly limitations and for the first time in her life she was not only free to go running across the throne room, but her eyes were bright and shining again . . . Joy is not based on circumstances; joy is based on hope. When we adjust our focus off of this world and begin to focus it on eternity, we can see that her life, though short, was not without purpose . . . Live like eternity matters, because it does . . . She couldn't say a word but she is a vessel that God is using to proclaim His love (1 Corinthians 1:27) . . . We may desire to serve God, but sometimes God will move more powerfully if we sit still and let Him move (Psalm 46:10)."*

Our pastor, John Weathersby, closed the speaking portion of the service: *"What she sees and knows now, what she learned that Sunday morning, is the only hope that can power us through this life . . . We had a short time together with her, but her impact is powerful. She has brought people together from all over the world! Tori points us squarely, necessarily, and needfully to God. Like a telescope, Tori magnified God for us; something so small made something so magnificent feel so close . . . That's our Tori! I mourn my loss, but I celebrate her gain."*

Joy was abundant in that place. We were surrounded by dozens of family members and hundreds of friends from all over the country—over 450 people from sixteen states were in attendance. We know of at least one who decided to follow Jesus because of Tori's life, and we praise God for that new life!

The guest book wasn't a book, but rather a shadow box that is now filled with wooden hearts of various sizes with the names of those in attendance written on each one. Each guest received a bookmark, a navy-blue ribbon with a photo of Tori (lovingly made by one of her Team Tori supporters from New Mexico!), and Cheetos and Dum Dums in a beautiful package, hand wrapped by our friends and family in the days before the service. Tori would have been excited about that!

The bookmarks from the funeral home couldn't have been more perfect. We had asked if they could incorporate our favorite photo of her—the last one of her smiling—as well as giraffes. Their graphic designer sent us many versions from which to choose, and it was so meaningful to us that they took the time to do so. Hetrick-Bitner handled all of these details exceedingly well, and we were so blessed by that.

Our photographer friends—Katie Bingaman, Sarah Benner (Brennan's cousin), Shannon Thornton, and Michelle Morrison—were happy to take photos throughout the day so that it would be well documented, as the rest of her life was. It was a relief to me to know that they would capture all of the details of the day so that I wouldn't have to be the one photographing it. Our friend, Micah Byler, also served us by filming the service as part of the continuing documentary he has been creating on Tori's life and impact.

Her celebration of life was the greatest party I have ever attended. As I led worship that day, I stood in awe of our great God and at the attendance—the impact our twenty-month-old daughter had, and will continue to have, is simply unbelievable. That God can use even babies to change lives is a true testimony to His power and love for all of us.

One of our littlest listeners died this morning—Easter morning.

Her name is Victoria, or "Tori," for short.

She loved her giraffe.

She had wonderful parents. Brennan and Lesa knew they would not have her long. So they made a "bucket list" for her, which included meeting us. This just happens to be the single biggest honor we've ever received.

She had Krabbe leukodystrophy, and her parents have written beautifully and profoundly about her struggles and their journey. You can find out more here: Tori's Triumph—Team Tori.

She passed away this morning at 9:05. That's her last photo, with her stuffed giraffe. Her mom says, "Those big eyes are open wide in heaven today."

That it happened while so many were celebrating God's ultimate victory over death reminds me, again, of the only source of hope in the whole world. It so happens that the One who overcame death also promises, "The lame will leap like deer."

Tori got to do some neat stuff in her short life.

But you ain't seen nothin' yet.

Tori's "adult friend" Brant posted these words on his blog and on his Facebook page after I told him that Tori had gone to be with Jesus. Two days later, Brant unexpectedly spoke about Tori on his radio show, and his words serve as an encouragement to our hearts still today:

One of our littlest listeners died over the weekend: her name was Tori. She wasn't quite two years old. It's hard for me to talk about, but it was such a big honor because her parents knew they wouldn't have her for long. She was born with a disease, diagnosed with it—they knew she probably wouldn't make it to two years old. So they made a bucket list for her, Brennan and Lesa, her parents, and they put on the bucket list "Meet Brant and Sherri"—which is, like, the biggest honor this show has ever gotten. So we got to meet Tori and hang out with her. I got to meet her a couple of times—what a sweetheart. She loved her stuffed giraffe and all giraffe-themed things, and her parents have done such a great job about letting people know about this disease that she has suffered from. Look up Team Tori on Facebook if you want to follow.

But one thing struck me: this was on Easter morning. Their daughter passed away at 9:05 a.m., and her parents were so thankful for the time they got to spend with her, and so thankful that she—who couldn't run around like other little girls, she couldn't toddle around, she couldn't do things—that now she can. And I love that about knowing God. Because they have their faith in who Jesus is, this was a sorrowful joy. I mean, I don't know what you would do without faith in God in that moment. Here they are, thinking, Look we believe in a God on Easter morning who conquered death. Without that I don't know what we have. We believe in that same God who said that in his kingdom, when He establishes it fully, the lame will leap like deer. And so, a little girl like her gets to do all the stuff a little girl should do. So they had this little bucket list for her and she did some really wonderful things, but I'm thinking, long term, she's just getting started now. Now she's having some fun. And how wonderful is it that we can say that? Without God, I don't know what there is to say!

Amen, Brant. She's just getting started.

In addition to the amazing support shown at her celebration, in the media, and on social media, we also saw a visible showing of support through two balloon releases that were held in her honor—one in Brennan's hometown of Mifflintown, Pennsylvania, and one in my hometown of Red Bluff, California. Balloons were also released all over the country in her honor, and we felt so loved. We attended the one in Mifflintown, wearing Tori's giraffe headbands ourselves. As hundreds of purple balloons were released into the air, the most fitting songs possible were playing over the sound system. There weren't many dry eyes on the field as we said "farewell" collectively to our beautiful girl. It was a perfect way to celebrate her.

43 Our New Normal

Background Music:
"We Are Yours," by I Am They

God is still good, sovereign, and faithful, despite the circumstances
we see around us, and is therefore worthy to be praised.
—HEATHER ZEMPEL, *AMAZED AND CONFUSED*

The wind gently swirled around the wind chimes, filling the air with their beautiful music. Other than the chimes, the house was quiet, an ever-present reminder of Tori's absence.

It was the first day that I was by myself at home, the first day of my "new life" without Tori by my side and no one else around. My dad had spent two extra weeks with us to help with some projects, and when he went home, it was just Brennan and me for the first time in over a month. I sipped my coffee and made a long list of things I had been neglecting for so long. Though the list was daunting, it was also an encouragement to me that I had plenty to do and I would not be bored. I began to write more to attempt to process all that had happened:

> Death is weird. It's unnatural. God never intended for death to happen (as we see in the book of Genesis), especially not the death of children. Some of the tasks I had to complete were not sad, but they were weird. Things like removing Tori from our health insurance. Realizing that next year we won't get a tax deduction for having a child anymore (thanks, IRS, for that subtle reminder that our child is dead). Returning her handicap

placard to PennDOT because she is no longer disabled. It's all just weird. The things that had become part of our daily life were removed from it in an instant.

Today our new life begins. A life without Tori. A life with new purpose and priorities. The visitors have stopped, the mail has slowed, the house is quiet. Tori has been a resident of heaven for a month now. My dad has returned to California after being here for five weeks total. It's just the two of us now.

Today is the third first day of our new life together.

11.06.10: We said "I do" and our life together began

07.30.14: Victoria Ruth was born and our life as a family began

04.26.16: Our life without Tori—just the two of us again—officially begins

I sit at the dining room table making a list of all the things that I need to accomplish while I sing along to some new favorite worship songs and drink my second cup of coffee.

We are taking some time to not only focus on our marriage but on our individual selves. This is especially important for me because I now have to establish a new routine, new objectives, and, really, a new life. The past two years were primarily focused on Tori and I selflessly poured all my effort and energy into her care.

How do I even begin to focus on myself now?

We decided that I won't be trying to find an official job in this interim between Tori and whatever comes next. I have lobbying to do, and we hope to have more children in a year or two, so I need to remain home.

It's so strange to be able to build a daily routine that involves only me—I have to answer questions such as "how do I want to fill my days?" Wisely. I have a few priorities right now: lobbying for newborn screening, writing a book, getting healthy (including losing all of my "sitting on a couch for fourteen months" weight), spending time in the Word, learning to love to cook again, playing piano and guitar, and continuing to maintain our home and garden. I'm so thankful for our careful budgeting and frugality that allow us to live on one income so well.

We have planned some trips this year and we are looking forward to our adventures and to spending quality time with one another. I have no desire to fill my calendar and be "busy" every day—in fact, I am forcing myself to allow plenty of time to just "be" and to continue to process all that has happened.

My heart aches for my baby girl and I know that will never go away. But as much as I long with all my heart to have her back with us, I know that she is where she is supposed to be. Where we ALL (as followers of Jesus) are supposed to be one day.

One day at a time I will establish new routines and take care of myself and our home. The Lord has brought us this far and I know that He will continue to lead us well. We trust Him with our past, present, and future, and we are thankful for His loving and gracious care.

"I will turn their mourning into joy. I will comfort them and exchange their sorrow for rejoicing."
—Jeremiah 31:13

44 _For Such a Time as This . . ._

"If you keep quiet at a time like this, deliverance and relief for the Jews will arise from some other place . . . Who knows if perhaps you were made queen for just such a time as this?"
—ESTHER 4:14

This might surprise you, but I have always liked to go unnoticed. I can sing the national anthem regularly in front of ten thousand people without being nervous but don't like to talk to anyone afterward. I enjoy leading the music part of a worship service but don't want to receive any attention from doing so. Part of that is an introvert trait, but I think the rest comes from a lack of confidence. I have always tended toward black and neutral clothing and shied away from colors and prints, hoping that no one would notice my extra pounds. I'm sure there are more examples, but these are the most obvious.

I have been timid about owning my talents and being confident in my giftings. I am a great vocalist and very musical but would never confidently tell anyone about that, as I was always nervous about being perceived as cocky or arrogant. I am a photographer, a writer, a musician. God has so richly blessed me in so many ways, yet I have lacked confidence. I always compared myself to others and would let my confidence be affected by the talents others possessed. I have always known that I was good at writing but never considered myself to be a writer, because that seemed to be an arrogant thing to call myself.

Likewise, I have struggled with feeling competitive toward other women, especially when in leadership positions with them. It was as if

I felt threatened by their giftings instead of trying to find the ways they complemented mine. On two mission trips—one where I was not a leader and another where I was a co-leader—I ended up inadvertently creating tension because I felt threatened by the other female leader and was afraid that my offerings wouldn't be fully valued or appreciated.

Like Paul said, "I do what I don't want to do . . ." I didn't want to be this way but I couldn't put a name to what was causing me to do so. I worked best with men as opposed to other women because of this "inferiority complex"—men are in a different category altogether, so I didn't feel threatened by them. That is likely why I always envisioned myself with sons as opposed to daughters.

For whatever reason, after Tori was diagnosed, I no longer felt insecure. I didn't notice it at first, but when I would go shopping for myself (a rarity), I found that I was buying colorful clothing and prints. I cared so much about the three of us coordinating clothing for Easter 2015—so unlike me—and that was likely because I knew it would be our only Easter as a family and I wanted it to be perfect.

After she died, I became bolder in many respects. Unafraid. I realized that it is okay to be confident—yet humble—about the talents God has given to me and that I didn't need to compare myself to other women. I felt free.

There are a few friends of mine who appear to have it all together, whose homes are always neat and well decorated for each season. I would feel inferior—even during the time with Tori where all I was doing was trying to survive each day—because their gifts were not my own. They appeared to be "the perfect wife and mother" while I was just trying to make it to dinnertime. However, I no longer feel that way. Perhaps because I had just lived through a parent's worst nightmare and survived.

For as long as I could remember, I had been praying to be able to write a song but it had always eluded me. I assumed that it wasn't my gifting and, as usual, my lack of confidence kept me from trying. Ten years prior to Tori's passing, I had developed a chord progression that I used for warming up on the guitar; in October 2015, a melody flowed out of my heart and I was that much closer to finally being able to write a song. And in July 2016, God answered that prayer: the words came easily and I finally wrote a song! I wrote it out of the depth of emotion I felt right after

Tori's diagnosis, but also as a reminder to anyone who hears it that God is in control and loves us.

Lord, Remind Me

I know it's for Your glory, Lord
But, I don't yet understand
My heart is so worn
This journey's been long
This valley's too much to bear

God, I know You're good
And I know You're love
And I know You never fail
So, why should I doubt?
Can't figure it out
Lord, please remind me now

Remind me, Lord
that things are not as they seem
That You're the God who heals
Restores and redeems
And Your grace abounds here
There is nothing to fear
God, I surrender all
Remind me, Lord

When life is hard
You pierce through the dark
Your love brings such joy to me
Lord, heal my heart
Shattered and torn
My life is an offering

It's so easy to see
When all's well around me

That You love me and lead my way
But, when sorrow and grief
Overwhelm me
Lord, please remind me

This world is not my home
I wasn't made for this
So I have to believe
Lord, help me see
That You're holding me in Your hand
That You have a plan

(You can find this song for free at noisetrade.com/lesabrackbill.)

I began my collegiate experience at Azusa Pacific University in 2001, pursuing a degree in vocal performance with a Spanish minor. I realized only one semester into the program that majoring in music would be a terrible thing for me to do—not because I wasn't talented enough to make it, but because I was already extremely critical of music and musicians, and I knew that studying it intensely would likely take the joy of music away from me. This probably isn't true for most music majors, but I knew it would be true for me.

My passion for politics was instilled within me by my family—namely my dad and his dad—and by the movie *The American President*. That movie introduced me to the idea of lobbying. My passion was further reinforced the summer after high school by the self-arranged internship with a Christian / family values lobbying firm I had the privilege of having, as well as an amazing mock legislature camp I attended called City on The Hill. Those six weeks in Sacramento were eye-opening and provided me with amazing opportunities, such as testifying on a bill in front of a committee (in real life, not at the camp). I was able to actually lobby for/ against bills and I loved it. So, after I dropped my music major and Spanish minor, I decided to change my major to political science and my minor to history. I don't remember the specifics of how I chose them—it just made sense at the time. This seemed like the path I was meant to take. I graduated with a bachelor of arts degree in political science in May 2005 and was ready to take on the world.

During my senior year at APU, I had the opportunity to take the StrengthsFinder test and was amazed at how well it described me. My number one strength? Belief—I must be passionate about what I am doing. I have learned that if I am not passionate about something, I will lose interest and be ineffective. This is why I play seven instruments—I would get to a certain level, get bored, and move on. StrengthsFinder explained so much about who I am, and I use the results to this day.

When I made the decision to move to Harrisburg in March 2008, I began making connections with lobbying firms and eventually landed a job with one. I was so excited—finally on the way to doing my dream job! Except it wasn't my dream job. My boss was difficult and seemed to be impossible to please. The subject matter of our lobbying was not something about which I could even force myself to be passionate. And I never got the opportunity to try actual lobbying. I tried to do my best in my position, but I struggled. I was forced to quit less than a year later and I felt so relieved! But that year in politics showed me something else, too: I didn't want to do it anymore.

For a conservative Republican (who is becoming more Libertarian as time passes), the political climate has become brutal in many ways. I began to feel almost persecuted for my beliefs and it made me tired. Since then, I have largely ignored the political arena except for glancing over headlines to know a little about what is going on.

I am a completely different person than I was in 2001. Those who knew me then have been surprised to see me almost running away from politics when all I wanted back then was to be in office. In the past few years, I have often wondered if I studied the wrong subjects in college, if I wasted my time getting a degree I would never use—a degree for which we are still paying. I have often questioned that decision given my feelings toward politics today. My time at APU was well-spent, though, as it made me who I am today in so many ways, and I still love my alma mater, even if I don't use my degree.

Fast-forward to February 13, 2015:

Tori is diagnosed with Krabbe—our baby is dying of a disease that could have been treated if they had found it at birth. We find out that only two states actually tested at the time (New York and Missouri—in the time since, Kentucky, Tennessee, Ohio, and Illinois also began screening) and only a handful more had legislation in place to eventually test.

We learn that it comes down to money for most states and that they won't add the test because it is such a rare disease . . . It would "only save a few lives."

Rare shouldn't mean ignored. Rare shouldn't be tossed aside because it isn't common. Every life matters.

It occurred to me that maybe this is why I have the degree that I have, that maybe everything has prepared me to lobby for lysosomal storage disorders like Krabbe to be screened for at birth. It just makes sense. I am certainly not the only one fighting for this and I won't be the last. Most Krabbe families are very active in pursuing legislation in their respective states, and Hunter's Hope works fervently for this cause. But I can't let my education, career experience, and my own personal connection to this go to waste if it can all be used for a greater good and ultimately save lives. I'm not perfect, and I'm pretty rusty when it comes to politics, but I am going to let my newfound confidence prevail and try to make a difference however I can.

I am passionate about Tori. I am passionate about how much I hate Krabbe. I hate what Krabbe took from our daughter, and I hate that it took her from us. So fighting for newborn screening comes naturally to me—the passion and fire are there and they will never be extinguished. Do I want to reenter politics? No way. Do I know the game? Yes, I do. Do I think I could be effective? With God's help, yes.

And we know that God causes everything to work together for the good of those who love God and are called according to his purpose for them.
—Romans 8:28

I don't know what God has planned, but I do know that He doesn't waste experiences. Everything can be used for His greater plan. And if this is what He has in store for me, then so be it. I'm all in.

♡

Shortly after Tori's diagnosis, I discovered that Pennsylvania had recently passed a law that added Krabbe to the state's newborn screening panel. It was nicknamed Hannah's Law after Hannah Ginion, a Krabbe warrior from the Philadelphia area. This law was passed in 2014 and was supposed to be enacted in December of that same year. It has yet to be fully implemented.

When I discovered that Pennsylvania had a law in place (shortly after Tori's diagnosis), I was slightly disappointed because I had so hoped to get a law in place in her name. I was happy there was one, of course, but in my desperation at the time, I wanted Tori's legacy to be a law in her name.

At times during our journey I became slightly jealous of the attention some of the other Krabbe children were receiving in the media. Every parent wants their child to "be someone," and given our circumstances, I sometimes fell into that mentality. God quickly reminded me that Tori's worth is not determined by her fame, the number of Facebook followers she has, or having her name attached to a law. She is valuable because she is His creation, His treasured child; her value comes from God alone as a beautiful creation of His, and from the love of her family. We decided that since Hannah got the law passed, now we were going to fight for the implementation.

So we began to ask questions of the Department of Health, and with the help of Anna Grantham at Hunter's Hope, we began to decipher the confusing way that Pennsylvania operates, because its newborn screening program is different than any other state, and it's very antiquated.

This is what we learned:

- Rather than having one panel of diseases for which all babies are tested, there are two panels, one with nine diseases (as of 2017)—called the mandatory panel—and one with twenty-six (called the follow-up panel).
- Each hospital is required to screen for the diseases on the mandatory panel and the state pays for those tests; but each hospital is required to absorb the cost of the follow-up panel, so they are allowed to

choose which diseases they test for. Essentially, this means that your zip code determines life or death if you are born with a rare genetic disorder like Krabbe, because a rural hospital won't have the same budget as a large city hospital.

- As of August 2017, Penn State Milton S. Hershey Medical Center is the only hospital in the entire state automatically testing for all six of the lysosomal storage disorders in Hannah's Law. This meant a lot to us since this is where Tori was diagnosed, and at least two others before her within three years.

- The Department of Health instituted an "advisory panel" for newborn screening, which advises the secretary of health about newborn screening. This panel is comprised of doctors from various fields of study from around the state and meets quarterly in Harrisburg.

The panel had a meeting about two weeks after Tori's celebration of life, so my dad and I went, and I was able to speak at the end of the meeting. Krabbe was on the agenda and had been addressed at the very beginning, but because I was only a member of the public, I had to wait until the very end—five hours later—to address the panel. I spoke passionately for over five minutes about why Krabbe should be added to Pennsylvania's mandatory panel and refuted all of the reasons against screening that had been given during the meeting. Afterward, the chair of the panel, who was known at the time to be against adding Krabbe to the panel, approached me and told me he disagreed with everything I said, but that we were on the same page with newborn screening. Sure we are. Thankfully since then he has come to be much more supportive of adding Krabbe to the mandatory panel and for that we are grateful.

In late June 2016, I had the opportunity to meet with the physician general of Pennsylvania as well as Representative Angel Cruz and others at the state capitol and found myself in great company there. They are passionate about seeing this law implemented as quickly as possible, and they want to completely reform Pennsylvania's two-panel system!

Since then, I have continued to attend each meeting of the advisory panel and continue to advocate passionately. Dr. Escolar published a crucial paper in September that may very well pave the way for most—if not all—states to add Krabbe to their screening panels. Pennsylvania's next meeting is in December and we are praying that this paper will have had an impact.

It has been a long road, but we believe that Pennsylvania will be screening every newborn for Krabbe in the coming year or two; until then, we will continue to fight.

45 What Might Have Been

Background Music:
"Glorious Unfolding," by Steven Curtis Chapman

I try not to think about what might have been, 'cause that was then . . .
We can't go back again; there's no use giving in,
and there's no way to know what might have been.
—LITTLE TEXAS, "WHAT MIGHT HAVE BEEN"

Before Tori was born, many people told us to cherish the early years because they would go quickly, never to return. After she was diagnosed with Krabbe, the moments moved faster and there was nothing we could do to stop the momentum. The days were fleeting, and we wondered each day how much more time we had with our beloved daughter.

As a photographer, it was natural for me to take thousands (more like tens of thousands) of photos of Tori, every angle and perspective possible, hoping that I could remember everything once she was gone.

But, the problem is that what can't be captured on film is what I miss the most. I couldn't capture how it felt to hold her—something I did for hours each and every day. How it felt to feel her breathing. Her smell. The touch of her soft, smooth skin.

I couldn't capture her soul, the very thing that makes us who we are.

Miss Tori has been with Jesus in heaven for nearly two years now and it is still strange. The impact she had on my life is still being discovered moment by moment, and I continue to be overwhelmed by gratitude more than any other emotion.

I think of her almost every waking minute. I now understand what my dad has said my entire life—that I am always on his mind. I don't even try to think about Tori—it just happens.

Recently, Brennan and I sat down together and watched many of the pre-Krabbe videos we have of her. Hearing her talk and laugh, watching her move freely, and remembering our precious girl before Krabbe took over her defenseless brain brought joy to our hearts. She had the BEST personality, even before she turned five months old.

And I'm still *grateful*. Her memory brings me joy, not pain. Peace, not grief. The *knowledge* (it's more than just a "belief" as that word is commonly used today) that we will be reunited with her one day brings such excitement to both of our hearts. It won't be that long in light of eternity!

Tori's earthly life was cut short, but this life is just the beginning for all of us anyway. The suggested song at the beginning of this chapter has amazing lyrics filled with truth—please take time to look up the song and lyrics. They are so meaningful, especially knowing that Steven Curtis Chapman has also lost a child and his words reflect his experience.

We're still doing well. The fourteen months of preparation for Tori's death certainly have helped in the months (and soon, years) that followed without her physically with us. We're still surprised by how easy it is to leave the house now and how lightly we can pack, how quiet our home is without the humming of machines, how free we feel due to the lack of a strict schedule.

We have our moments where missing her is something we feel physically. A great example of this was when I first heard the song "Eye of the Storm" by Ryan Stevenson and I was caught off guard by this line: "When a sickness takes my child away and there's nothing I can do, my only hope is to trust in You." Powerful truth.

Sometimes it comes out of nowhere; other times it comes out of thoughtful remembrance of our adventures with her. We've both shed tears during those moments.

But because of God and who He is, we are hopeful above all else and remain joyful. God is doing amazing things and is still using our little girl to change lives, even after her death. Tori was a remarkable little girl and her legacy lives on. We have MUCH to be thankful for and will continue to focus on those blessings rather than her absence.

Those tens of thousands of photographs continue to make us smile as we remember the incredible life we lived with Tori, and we will continue living life abundantly until we are reunited with her forever. It will be worth the wait.

A passage often mentioned and referenced when going through trials is James 1:2–4:

> *Dear brothers and sisters, when troubles of any kind come your way, consider it an opportunity for great joy. For you know that when your faith is tested, your endurance has a chance to grow. So let it grow, for when your endurance is fully developed, you will be perfect and complete, needing nothing.*

I've always assumed that these verses were referring to the perspective and attitude we should have during the trials; however, perhaps the joy is actually a joy deferred, for once you have endured trials and tragedy, the appreciation and joy you experience in life afterward is magnified greatly.

My pregnancy with Tori wasn't always joyful; and, subsequently, losing her was tragic and heartbreaking. However, the joy I will experience with future children will be amplified by the tragedy of losing Tori. Every milestone, every accomplishment—even the simple fact that they are alive and well will fill my heart with such joy, a joy that I would never have found had I not been Tori's mother.

So, I believe that the statement in James can be interpreted in two ways: one, find joy when going through trials because of your faith that God is at work and that He has a plan and purpose; two, recognize that your future joy will be even greater because of what you have endured.

Trials are an opportunity for God to work mightily in our lives, even if we can't see the why or the how in the moment.

It's so easy to let our minds run away from us and to ponder what might have been instead of what actually is. If we aren't careful, we can make ourselves incredibly sad on days like Tori's birthday instead of celebrating that she is healed and with Jesus. We could focus on all that she might be doing as a healthy child here on earth, or we can imagine her healed, whole, healthy body running around in heaven where we will see her again (soon, but not quite yet, as Jim Kelly has said).

Brennan and I have learned that you must take control of your thoughts in times like this—not that you can't grieve, of course, but don't force yourself into sadness simply because you are wondering about what may have been. It doesn't change anything, it doesn't benefit you in any way, and it doesn't bring joy. In fact, it steals joy.

Even though terrible things happen, find joy in the midst. Look for God at work.

We continue to remember the great times we had with Tori. We are thinking about what happened instead of what could have happened if she had been healthy. And our joy is REAL. It is genuine. It is God-given. There is such peace in knowing that she is running around with Jesus and those who have gone before us. She breathes normally, her nerves don't cause her pain, and her body is whole. And that knowledge is the best possible gift we could ever receive.

Thank You, Jesus, for Your peace and joy, and Thank You for making us Tori's parents.

46 Heaven and What Will Be

Background Music:
"You Never Let Go," by Matt Redman

All their life in this world and all their adventures in Narnia had only been the cover and the title page: now at last they were beginning Chapter One of the Great Story which no one on earth has read: which goes on for ever: in which every chapter is better than the one before.
—C. S. Lewis, *The Last Battle*, p. 767

Death is not a popular subject of conversation in most circles, not even in church. As humans, we seem to prefer to believe that we are going to live forever here when, in reality, this life on earth is very short in light of eternity.

As it became increasingly apparent that the Lord was not going to choose to heal Tori on earth, it forced us to think about death and heaven far more than we had ever done. We began to ask questions like, What is heaven like? What does the Bible tell us about our future home? Why do believers mourn as the world does, when we know that our separation is only temporary?

I believe that we, as Christians, have allowed the enemy to persuade us that death is the end, that death is scary, that death is devastating, when the Bible repeatedly reminds us that it isn't. I am not saying that it is wrong to be sad when a loved one dies. Rather, I think we forget that death is only the beginning and we grieve as if we have no hope of seeing our loved ones again.

Paul writes this in 1 Thessalonians 4:13:

> *And now, dear brothers and sisters, we want you to know what will happen to the believers who have died so you will not grieve like people who have no hope.*

And in 2 Corinthians 4:8–10 and 16–18 he writes,

> *We are pressed on every side by troubles, but we are not crushed. We are perplexed, but not driven to despair. We are hunted down, but never abandoned by God. We get knocked down, but we are not destroyed. Through suffering, our bodies continue to share in the death of Jesus so that the life of Jesus may also be seen in our bodies . . . That is why we never give up. Though our bodies are dying, our spirits are being renewed every day. For our present troubles are small and won't last very long. Yet they produce for us a glory that vastly outweighs them and will last forever! So we don't look at the troubles we can see now; rather, we fix our gaze on things that cannot be seen. For the things we see now will soon be gone, but the things we cannot see will last forever.*

In 2 Corinthians 5:1–9 he continues:

> *For we know that when this earthly tent we live in is taken down (that is, when we die and leave this earthly body), we will have a house in heaven, an eternal body made for us by God himself and not by human hands. We grow weary in our present bodies, and we long to put on our heavenly bodies like new clothing. For we will put on heavenly bodies; we will not be spirits without bodies. While we live in these earthly bodies, we groan and sigh, but it's*

> *not that we want to die and get rid of these bodies that clothe us. Rather, we want to put on our new bodies so that these dying bodies will be swallowed up by life. God himself has prepared us for this, and as a guarantee he has given us his Holy Spirit.*
>
> *So we are always confident, even though we know that as long as we live in these bodies we are not at home with the Lord. For we live by believing and not by seeing. Yes, we are fully confident, and we would rather be away from these earthly bodies, for then we will be at home with the Lord. So whether we are here in this body or away from this body, our goal is to please him.*

Notice that Paul refers to our earthly bodies as tents and our bodies in heaven as houses. Which is better? Which is built to last?

Another time Paul mentions death is in Philippians 1:21–23: *"For to me, living means living for Christ, and dying is even better. But if I live, I can do more fruitful work for Christ. So I really don't know which is better. I'm torn between two desires: I long to go and be with Christ, which would be far better for me."* We're meant to be with Jesus!

After Tori made her way to heaven, Brennan and I began to study the book *Heaven* by Randy Alcorn to learn about Tori's new home and our future one. It has forever changed our perspective on life, on death, and on eternity.

As believers, we should long for heaven far more than we cling to this earth. The unknown is scary, but if we truly trust in God and who He is, we will believe Him in this, as well.

The book *The Last Battle* of The Chronicles of Narnia paints a great analogy of what heaven will be like based on what we know from the Bible:

> *"Why, they're exactly like. Look, there's Mount Pire with his forked head, and there's the pass into Archenland and everything!"*
>
> *"And yet they're not like," said Lucy. "They're different. They have more colours on them and they look further away than*

> I remembered and they're more . . . more . . . oh, I don't know . . ."
>
> "More like the real thing," said Lord Digory softly. (p. 759)
>
> "When Aslan said you would never go back to Narnia, he meant the Narnia you were thinking of. But that was not the real Narnia. That had a beginning and an end. It was only a shadow or copy of the real Narnia which has always been here and always will be here: just as our own world, England and all, is only a shadow or copy of something in Aslan's real world. You need not mourn over Narnia, Lucy. All of the old Narnia that mattered, all the dear creatures, have been drawn into the real Narnia through the Door. And of course it is different; as different as a real thing is from a shadow or as waking life is from a dream." (p. 759)
>
> "You may have been in a room in which there was a window that looked out on a lovely bay of the sea or a green valley that wound away among mountains. And in the wall of that room opposite to the window there may have been a looking-glass. And as you turned away from the window you suddenly caught sight of that sea or that valley, all over again, in the looking glass. And the sea in the mirror, or the valley in the mirror, were in one sense just the same as the real ones: yet at the same time they were somehow different—deeper, more wonderful, more like places in a story: in a story you have never heard but very much want to know." (p. 760)

Earth is all we have ever known. It is our home; it is where we have loved deeply, lived abundantly, and experienced joy and laughter. But as Lewis says, this earth is a mere shadow of what heaven is like. In heaven there are no more tears, no sorrow, no pain, no regret, no hate. This earth is broken, decaying, filled with evil, and it will come to an end. And yet we don't want to leave it. We trust what we see more than we trust the One who created it all. We fear death instead of longing for heaven.

When God created the earth, He made it perfectly and man was created to live forever. However, when sin entered the world through Adam and Eve, so did death. Death, pain, broken relationships, and sin hurt our hearts deeply because they aren't supposed to exist—it wasn't God's plan! Because God cannot be in the presence of sin, in His mercy He assigned a lifespan to humans and began His plan of redemption. If He hadn't done this, we would have been separated from Him forever. He loves us too much to allow that.

We live daily with the assurance that Tori is more alive now than she ever was.

Tori was present on earth for 607 days. One year, seven months, and twenty-seven days.

Yet she will be in heaven for eternity. And so will we. Why would we want to be anywhere else?

> *But, Lord, 'tis for Thee, for Thy coming we wait,*
> *The sky, not the grave, is our goal;*
> *Oh, trump of the angel! Oh, voice of the Lord!*
> *Blessed hope, blessed rest of my soul!*

> *And Lord, haste the day when the faith shall be sight,*
> *The clouds be rolled back as a scroll;*
> *The trump shall resound, and the Lord shall descend,*
> *Even so, it is well with my soul.*
> —HORATIO SPAFFORD, "IT IS WELL WITH MY SOUL"

My grandfather, Papa Fay, passed away in June 2015 after a long battle with Alzheimer's disease. He was the first (and only, thus far) grandparent I had lost—something I do not take for granted. His death taught me so much, and though I didn't recognize it at the time, it prepared me for Tori's passing nine months later.

We watched him decline as the horrible disease overtook his faculties, and we prayed for years that the Lord would take him home so that he wouldn't suffer any longer on this earth. When he went to heaven on June

10, 2015, he was no longer the man any of us had known and loved—he was merely a shell, a body.

But his death brought us *joy* because we knew for certain that he had a relationship with Jesus and that He was now present with the Lord in heaven. He could visit with people (his favorite thing to do, a joy that the disease robbed from him as time passed), he could walk, sing, dance, and express himself. He was FREE from the chains of Alzheimer's disease at last, and we know that we will one day be reunited with him for eternity. *What hope and joy that knowledge brings!*

As we watched Tori decline and saw Krabbe taking a strong hold of her precious little body, this experience with Papa Fay brought me such comfort. She was no longer the baby we once had, and her brain was gradually losing the ability to function well. If God wasn't going to heal her here on earth, we were comforted by the knowledge that He would heal her in heaven.

After all, God's Word tells us this about heaven:

> *He will wipe every tear from their eyes, and there will be no more death or sorrow or crying or pain. All these things are gone forever. (Revelation 21:4)*

When we—as followers of Jesus—are living with eternity in mind, our earthly perspective on death will shift from sorrow to joy.

How is this possible?

We all know that death is inevitable—Scripture (and life experience) makes that clear.

> *For everything there is a season,*
> *a time for every activity under heaven.*
> *A time to be born and a time to die.*
> *(Ecclesiastes 3:1–2a)*
>
> *And I know you are sending me to my death—*
> *the destination of all who live. (Job 30:23)*
>
> *None of us can hold back our spirit from departing. None of us*
> *has the power to prevent the day of our death. (Ecclesiastes 8:8)*

BUT, we also know that this earth isn't our home; it isn't where we belong.

Death is NOT the end of our existence.

We are only here for a short time to form a relationship with God and to preach the Gospel to all so that all might be saved through Him. We are here to prepare for eternity.

None of us are guaranteed tomorrow:

> *Look here, you who say, "Today or tomorrow we are going to*
> *a certain town and will stay there a year. We will do business*
> *there and make a profit."* **How do you know what your life**
> **will be like tomorrow?** *Your life is like the morning fog—it's*
> *here a little while, then it's gone. What you ought to say is, "If*
> *the Lord wants us to, we will live and do this or that." (James*
> *4:13–15; emphasis mine)*
>
> *Don't brag about tomorrow, since you don't know what the day*
> *will bring. (Proverbs 27:1)*

Since we aren't going to live on this earth forever, why do we allow ourselves to become so sad when our loved ones who knew Jesus depart for heaven?

Another truth that has brought us peace is this: God knows how many days we will live on this earth. He knows and isn't surprised by death! Nothing is out of His control, so there is no reason for us to feel guilty or as though we didn't do enough. Indeed, He knew that Tori was going to join Him on March 27, 2016, no matter where we were or what we may have done to stop it.

> *You have decided the length of our lives. You know how many*
> *months we will live, and we are not given a minute longer.*
> —JOB 14:5

> *You saw me before I was born. Every day of my life was recorded in*
> *your book. Every moment was laid out before a single day had passed.*
> —PSALM 139:16

The knowledge that the sovereign God of the universe cares greatly about the details of our lives brings such comfort and peace to my soul.

I have been blessed with a few wise women in my life, women who love the Lord and whose words are gentle and timely. These friends are worth more than gold and I'm so grateful for their presence in my life. Recently I had the opportunity to sit and visit with my friend Rachel Gunsauls. I have known Rachel since middle school and she has been a source of encouragement and comfort throughout this entire journey with Tori, always praying for us and texting/e-mailing me notes of encouragement just when I needed them the most.

As we sat in her beautiful backyard, surrounded by oak trees and golden waves of grass, our conversation veered toward God and His Word as it usually does. As we talked about Tori's heaven-going, I mentioned that I try to always say it like that—heaven-going—instead of "death" or "passing away," because that's the truth. That's where she is.

Rachel remarked that she thinks that Christians should have an entirely different term for death / passing away than the world does because we KNOW that those who believe in Jesus as their Lord and Savior are in heaven. They aren't just gone; they didn't cease to exist entirely—they are in their eternal home, the one in which we as believers will reside someday, as well. It's not good-bye; it's "see you soon!" This should bring us JOY!

> *"Don't let your hearts be troubled. Trust in God, and trust also in me.* There is more than enough room in my Father's home. If this were not so, would I have told you that I am going to prepare a place for you? When everything is ready, I will come and get you, so that you will always be with me where I am. And you know the way to where I am going."
>
> "No, we don't know, Lord," Thomas said. "We have no idea where you are going, so how can we know the way?"
>
> Jesus told him, **"I am the way, the truth, and the life. No one can come to the Father except through me."** (John 14:1–6; emphasis mine)

Jesus told us He was going to prepare a place for us and that we would one day join Him there. If we believe His Word to be true, we should believe Him in this, as well. He said we shouldn't allow our hearts to be troubled with things of this world but to trust Him instead.

And yet we allow the enemy to instill fear and long-lasting sorrow within us when our loved ones become residents in heaven . . .

Do we miss their presence in our earthly lives? *Of course*—they impacted us, we loved them, and now they aren't physically present. That's the sting of death that Paul mentions in 1 Corinthians 15:54–55. However, *they aren't really gone*—they are in the presence of our resurrected Savior and are made whole again! We must remind ourselves of this instead of being overtaken by sorrow and grief.

We are taught from birth that knowledge is power; wisdom is applying the knowledge we possess to our lives. *The knowledge that our loved ones who knew Jesus are in heaven is powerful and can aid in turning our mourning into dancing.*

The way that we combat the work of the enemy in any area of our lives is by applying and speaking truth into the situation. Occasionally, the enemy attempts to make me feel regret and guilt in regard to Tori's short life. In those moments, I halt those attempts by speaking truth: we lived life with Tori to the fullest and we cared for her in the best possible way. We have NO reason to have regrets or guilt!

Truth brings FREEDOM.

The enemy tries to make us feel afraid, overcome with sorrow, and filled with guilt and regret. He wants us to feel like failures, like we are unworthy of God's love and grace. When we remind ourselves of God's truth and His promises, we can overcome these things!

Our days are written in God's book before we are even born, so we shouldn't feel guilty about what we could have done. God knew this was the plan for Tori's life.

Speak truth in the middle of your fear and sorrow. Remind yourself that God is good, He is faithful, He is sovereign. He loves you and IS love. *He is still God* even when you can't see His hand working.

One of the truths I remember daily is that Tori is no longer confined in a broken body that couldn't function properly—as her mother, knowing that she is free makes me so happy! She has beaten Krabbe and has overcome it! The course of Krabbe in her life was inevitable, so the hope and joy of heaven is indescribable.

My cousin Jenn Eskridge shared this with me not long after Tori went to heaven: "*The pastor's son had lost his daughter at the age of 5. He said that when he went to visit her, he called the gravesite her resurrection site, because that was where her earthly body was laid, but he knew God had already robbed that grave and brought her into her eternal home.*"

It is the same way with the resurrection of the dead. Our earthly bodies are planted in the ground when we die, but they will be raised to live forever. **Our bodies are buried in brokenness, but they will be raised in glory. They are buried in weakness, but they will be raised in strength. They are buried as natural human bodies, but they will be raised as spiritual bodies . . .**

. . .What I am saying, dear brothers and sisters, is that our physical bodies cannot inherit the Kingdom of God. These dying bodies cannot inherit what will last forever. But let me reveal to you a wonderful secret. We will not all die, but we will all be transformed! *It will happen in a moment, in the blink of an eye, when the last trumpet is blown. For when the trumpet sounds, those who have died will be raised to live forever. And we who are living will also be transformed. For our dying bodies must be transformed into bodies that will never die; our mortal bodies must be transformed into immortal bodies.*

Then, when our dying bodies have been transformed into bodies that will never die, this Scripture will be fulfilled:

> **"Death is swallowed up in victory.**
> **O death, where is your victory?**
> **O death, where is your sting?"**

For sin is the sting that results in death, and the law gives sin its power. But thank God! He gives us victory over sin and death through our Lord Jesus Christ.

So, my dear brothers and sisters, be strong and immovable. Always work enthusiastically for the Lord, for you know that nothing you do for the Lord is ever useless. *(1 Corinthians 15:42–44, 50–58; emphasis mine)*

It is often said that we tend to only believe God when it's easy. After all, it's easy to follow God when life is going well, when we have plenty, when things are comfortable.

As Job so beautifully demonstrated, God is STILL good and His word is still true even when we lose it all. He is still worthy of our praise and devotion even when we lose a child. And true faith follows even when the way is unclear.

We need to realize that God's Word is relevant in ALL parts of our lives, including death and other difficult times.

Do we believe the Bible or just parts of it that are convenient and easy?
What about when life is messy?

If we believe that the Bible is the holy Word of God Himself, how can we disregard the promises and hope He gives even through the difficult issues?

The Bible mentions death numerous times, and those verses are typically followed by a reminder of the hope that we have because of what Jesus did on the cross. Here's one example:

> And now, dear brothers and sisters, we want you to know what will happen to the believers who have died **so you will not grieve like people who have no hope** . . .
>
> . . . Then we will be with the Lord forever. So **encourage each other with these words.** (1 Thessalonians 4:13, 17–18; emphasis mine)

Paul tells us to ENCOURAGE each other about death in this passage. Death was never God's plan for us, but Adam and Eve changed the course of history and death became inevitable. One bite of the forbidden fruit (disobedience) brought death into the world.

> *We are geared for perfection, which is why we*
> *are always so disappointed in life.*
> —RACHEL GUNSAULS

And yet *death is not the end for any of us.* We are all born with eternal souls, and we make the choice during this life to follow Jesus or to walk away from Him—the latter of which results in an eternity in hell.

For those who have chosen Jesus, *we have no reason to fear death.* Death is merely the next step toward our eternal home, and we will be FREE of all of the issues this world contains. This world is not our home. One day we will be with Jesus Himself, forever, and that is great news! That alone is reason to rejoice always.

Romans tells us to be transformed by the renewing of our minds (12:2) and this happens when we embrace God's truth and allow it to transform us . . . this pertains to death as well!

Jesus told us not to *worry* (Matthew 6:34), not to be *afraid* (multiple times), and to remember that He has overcome the same world from which we wish to hide (John 16:33).

We are instructed to dwell on things above, not on earthly things:

> *Since you have been raised to new life with Christ, set your sights on the realities of heaven, where Christ sits in the place of honor at God's right hand. Think about the things of heaven, not the things of earth. For you died to this life, and your real life is hidden with Christ in God. And when Christ, who is your life, is revealed to the whole world, you will share in all his glory . . .*
>
> *Put on your new nature, and be renewed as you learn to know your Creator and become like him. (Colossians 3:1–4, 10)*

The world has no hope, but we do. And how is the world going to find the hope that we have if we don't live it out?

Let me encourage you with this:

Trust the Lord FULLY, even when you can't see what He's doing.

Remember that He has numbered our days and knows when we will leave this earth.

Don't wonder what might have been; don't have regrets.

Live life to the fullest NOW and focus on what matters—loving God and loving others.

Then you will have greater peace when a loved one goes to heaven before you.

I long for heaven more than ever before now that Tori is a resident of that wonderful place, and I am enjoying learning more about her current (and our future) home.

I know that someday we will be reunited FOREVER and will never be apart. The anticipation of that day brings such excitement, even though I have no idea how long it will be until we are reunited. All I know is that it will feel as if no time has passed at all since heaven doesn't operate within the time we know.

Does all of this mean that I shouldn't cry when I miss her? Of course not. Grief is natural and I will never stop missing her.

However, I do believe that having a biblical perspective on death and heaven eases the blow of her absence, and it brings me peace that cannot be otherwise explained.

Set your mind on things above . . . choose joy . . . be grateful . . . trust God.

Heaven, along with the knowledge that we'll be reunited with our loved ones (who also knew Jesus), removes the sting of death, one thorn at a time.

Praise Jesus for His grace and mercy that make any of this possible.

47 "Even Though . . ."

Background Music:
"All Along," by Remedy Drive

Even though the fig trees have no blossoms,
and there are no grapes on the vines;
even though the olive crop fails,
and the fields lie empty and barren;
even though the flocks die in the fields,
and the cattle barns are empty,
yet I will rejoice in the Lord!
I will be joyful in the God of my salvation!
The Sovereign Lord is my strength!
He makes me as surefooted as a deer,
able to tread upon the heights.
—HABAKKUK 3:17–19

Habakkuk 3:17–19 is not a new passage to me. It's one I considered many times throughout our journey with Tori because it applied so well to our situation. In this passage, Habakkuk, a prophet of God, states that no matter what happens, no matter how hard things become, he would rejoice in the Lord and be joyful. Heather Zempel's commentary on this book of the Bible—and on this passage, specifically—is excellent. From her book, *Amazed and Confused*:

> When Habakkuk came to a place where God's actions collided with his expectations, he found the only hopeful response was worship that was rooted in an unshakable and undeniable awareness of God's character, ways, and works. (p. 160)
>
> We can frame the character of God according to our circumstances, or we can frame our circumstances according to what we know of the character of God. We can let our circumstances inform what we know to be true of God or we can let what we know to be true about God inform our circumstances. As Warren Wiersbe said, "God doesn't always change the circumstances, but He can change us to meet the circumstances. That's what it means to live by faith." (pp. 178–9)

God continually reminded the Israelites of the importance of remembering all that He had done for them, and yet they continued to forget. When they weren't studying His word and their history, they lost sight of God's goodness and plan and they strayed from His will.

As we said at the beginning of our journey, God has never been unfaithful to us, so why would He be unfaithful now? Because we had reminded ourselves for years of His wonderful works since the beginning of time and of His works in our own lives, trusting Him with Tori came fairly easily.

> He works things together for His purpose and not our expectations. (p. 184)
>
> Sovereignty means that God is in charge. Eternally in charge. We need God to redefine our suffering against the background of eternity because eternity puts things into perspective. (p. 188)

When things don't go as we plan, do we run *from* God or *to* God? Why is it so easy for us to discard our faith just because things get tough? Why don't we trust His proven faithfulness to be present in our own lives?

This final quote is a great summary of our perspective on Tori's short life:

> *I refuse to let what I don't know keep me from*
> *worshiping what I do know. (p. 190)*

We KNOW that there is ONE true God. We know that God is sovereign, that He is good and loving and gracious. We KNOW that there is a heaven waiting for those who believe in and follow Jesus and that this life is only the beginning. We KNOW that He has written the number of days in His book and there's nothing we can do to change that. We are certain of these things!

We DON'T know why God chose us to be Tori's parents, why He allowed her to have Krabbe, or why He didn't choose to heal her on earth so that she could grow up under our care. We don't know what the future holds for us in regard to having more children—though we know those children will be impacted by Tori's life in ways we cannot even begin to imagine. But as that last quote says, we aren't going to let these few unknowns keep us from serving and praising the One who does know!

We know that He has a plan for us and that Tori is waiting for us in heaven. Whether or not God chooses to reveal to us His thoughts on this situation here or if we will find out in heaven, even so it is still well with our souls.

The depth of my love for my daughter is not measured by the number of tears I have cried, but rather by the life I choose to live in her absence. I choose to live a life of love, joy, peace, patience, kindness, goodness, and grace (Galatians 5:22). She deserves all of that, and more.

Our faith isn't blind, and it isn't a Band-Aid. Our faith is the lens through which we view this entire life, and it's the source of our joy and our peace, and it's the reason why we continue to praise God and choose joy "even though" we lost our only child.

After all, our loss doesn't change God's character or His purposes for us. He is *still* good.

> *If you have questions about this Jesus that we love and serve, please feel free to contact us through our blog (www.thebrackbills.com) or find a local pastor who can meet with you. It's the most important decision you will ever make.*

I have served as the worship leader at Transcend Church since January 2017. While I have led worship almost continually over the past twenty-two years in some capacity, this is the first time I have been "the leader" of a worship team instead of just playing guitar and singing. This has certainly been a growing experience for me and I am so thankful for the members of the worship team and their talents and hearts for worship.

Few are aware of what goes into choosing a worship set—it's far more than just picking songs you like. I typically read the Scripture for the upcoming sermon and prayerfully choose songs that go along with the sermon. Yet, sometimes it's honestly just following the Holy Spirit's guidance and how I "feel" about a song fitting in with the set.

One week in May was definitely a "feel" week as the passage did not easily lend itself to songs. While I was doing all of this, I considered that the Sunday for which I was preparing was Mother's Day but didn't give it much thought.

As I leafed through my (gigantic) binder of music, a few jumped out at me, unrelated in theme at first glance—"Great Is Thy Faithfulness" would start the morning as a great reminder that God is trustworthy, merciful, and faithful. We'd do "Even Unto Death" and "Give Me Faith" to remind ourselves that the God we serve is worthy to be followed and trusted, no matter what. I chose a few other songs to fill in the set and thought I was done.

I grabbed my guitar and began playing through the set, but it still didn't feel complete. Later that afternoon the hymn "It Is Well with My Soul"—one of my favorites—came into my head and I knew that was what was missing. In addition, I decided to add Bethel's song "It Is Well" to the end.

If you aren't aware, the backstory to the song "It Is Well" is one of the most powerful I've ever heard. Mr. Spafford lost his four daughters in a shipwreck, all at once. Four daughters. And yet, he penned the words to this poem (now song) and declared that it was well with his soul.

How can that be?

I contend that...

It can be well with your soul despite your grief.

It can be well with your soul despite your circumstances.

It can be well with your soul despite your questions and uncertainties of God's actions.

This can all be true because it isn't dependent on you—it's dependent on God. When you believe the truth of who God is (faithful, loving, merciful, kind, generous, good), when you believe His Word and His promises (there IS life after death for those who trust in Jesus!), and when you trust Him fully, there is peace within your soul that surpasses understanding (Philippians 4:7). We've lived it. We know this is true.

We have a beautiful sign in our home that quotes this hymn, and it has been a great reminder to us as we've learned to live without Tori here on earth. We've truly learned that "whatever our lot" may be, "even so" we can be at peace when we are trusting the Lord and following Him.

As I led worship that morning, the emotion of missing Tori began to well up inside as we sang the final verse of the hymn:

And Lord, haste the day when my faith shall be sight,
The clouds be rolled back as a scroll;
The trump shall resound, and the Lord shall descend,
Even so, it is well with my soul!

The emotion was twofold: first, remembering the tragic circumstances that brought this song into this world and how deep the pain is when you lose a child; second, I long for this day—the day when Jesus returns and we are reunited with our precious Tori (and other loved ones who have gone before us). I cannot wait for that day and for the eternity with her that will follow.

I got through the song, but as the sermon began my eyes were teary as I pondered the joyous reunion that awaits us.

As the Bethel song by the same name says,

Through it all, through it all, my eyes are on you.
Through it all, through it all, it is well.
So let go, my soul, and trust in Him;
The waves and wind still know His name.

The same Jesus who calmed the storm that threatened to wreck the ship He and His disciples were on is the same Jesus who lives today and loves us deeply. He is still in control, even when we can't feel it.

Being well in your soul doesn't mean that things are perfect, or that you pretend to not be in pain. It simply means that you trust Jesus more than you fear your circumstances.

Yes, my Tori is gone. Yes, my heart longs for her. Even so, it is well with my soul.

The hill from the employee parking lot to the building where we work is gigantic. It is long, steep, and, especially when it's cold outside, the prospect of walking up to work is daunting. Most days I am spoiled because Brennan drops me off at the entrance and then goes to park the van; but, on days when our schedules do not match, I am left to climb the mountain. And I don't want to do it most days.

The challenge is half psychological and half physical. I'm not in great shape—yet—so that's part of it. But when I look at the hill, I also have to convince my brain that I can do it, because it feels like I will never make it, like I will fail.

What I have found is this: if I focus on my feet and on taking one step at a time instead of looking up to the top of the hill, it is far less challenging. If I take it one step at a time, it's not that bad! I make it to the top of the hill, a little out of breath, but I can do it. I succeed.

This analogy is a perfect one for our lives right now: some days it seems like our hearts will never fully heal, that it will be forever before we are reunited with her again. We long to hold our baby girl and gaze into her beautiful eyes once more, and that time (and heaven) seems so far away.

But, when we take the journey one step at a time, focusing on the Lord and on one task at a time, it's so much easier and we feel refreshed. We don't feel overwhelmed or tired. We feel at peace and we know that we can take the next step. Why is it so hard to remember to do this?

Whatever your mountain might be today, focus on the next step, not on the entire climb. Allow the Lord to guide you and sustain you; He is faithful and will lead you well.

> *Give your burdens to the Lord, and he will take care of you.*
> *He will not permit the godly to slip and fall.*
> —PSALM 55:22

> *Give all your worries and cares to God, for he cares about you.*
> —1 PETER 5:7

Joy isn't always obvious; sometimes you have to fight for it, sometimes you have to search for it, but the journey toward a joy-filled life—especially when it seems impossible—is always worth it.

Afterword

I had hoped that I would be able to definitively say that Pennsylvania (and other states) were now screening for Krabbe at birth by the time this book was published, but that has not turned out to be true. The legislative battle is vitally important, and we will not rest until each state is giving every single child the best possible chance at life by screening them at birth for as many genetic diseases as possible.

Maryland and Pennsylvania are very close to implementing screening statewide and we look forward to that progress, small as it may seem.

We will continue to post updates on our blog (www.thebrackbills. com), and you can write to your legislators and see a current list of states that are screening at www.huntershope.org if you would like to help this cause.

If your state does not include Krabbe in its newborn screening program, you can order a supplemental screening kit through huntershope.org and take it with you to the hospital.

A Timeline of Events

Here is a brief timeline of what happened to illustrate how quickly Krabbe took over Tori's brain.

As we look back, we see more signs of the disease earlier, but we just didn't know what they were at the time. Lesson learned: if your child is not reaching milestones within the typical age range, it doesn't hurt to ask his or her doctor.

- **July 30, 2014:** Victoria Ruth Brackbill is born at 9:25 a.m. in Harrisburg, Pennsylvania.
- **October 1:** Tori has an ultrasound on her head due to the rapid growth; no issues found.
- **December 19:** Tori refuses to nurse and seems angry.
- **December 30:** Tori turns five months old. She still hates tummy time. She starts wanting to eat more frequently because she isn't eating enough at each feeding.
- **January 6, 2015:** The last picture of Tori smiling is taken.
- **January 7:** Tori's demeanor begins to change and she becomes more irritable; she also begins regressing in the areas of talking, smiling, playing with toys, and so forth, very rapidly. She throws up more frequently. She only wants to be held.
- **January 14:** We have our appointment with the pediatrician; reflux diagnosis is given. All symptoms align with reflux. Medication is started.
- **January 15:** Tori gets an upper GI X-ray done to check her intestines and bowels. All is clear.
- **January 21:** Day seven of reflux medicine with no improvement. Lesa calls the doctor again.
- **January 29:** Tori visits the pediatrician again; he suspects excess fluid in her head, and an MRI is scheduled for May 6. The doctor says she is in pain and wonders if it is migraines.

- **January 30:** Tori turns six months old. She doesn't eat well that day, so the pediatrician suggests going to the ER at Hershey Med to try to push for an MRI. CT scan is performed. Brain abnormalities are observed.
- **February 3:** Tori has her neurosurgeon appointment. Doctor pushes for MRI to be done the next day and succeeds. He is concerned about CT scan results and her developmental regression.
- **February 4:** The MRI is performed, and the neurosurgeon calls that afternoon to give us results.
- **February 5:** Tori gets routine vaccinations, and we show the pediatrician the MRI. He tells us to try to give her canned coconut milk to get fat into her body, because her body is clearly not absorbing any.
- **February 6:** We meet with the neurologist and she tells us that it appears to be a form of leukodystrophy. Tori does not eat all day and is dehydrated, so she is admitted to Hershey Med for a feeding tube.
- **February 6–11:** In the hospital. Tons of tests are done, including a swallow study, which shows that she is aspirating while eating, so the NG tube is going to stay. Blood work is drawn to determine which leukodystrophy she has.
- **February 13:** The neurologist calls and asks us to come in for the results: it's Krabbe disease. Our world is turned upside-down. That evening, another Krabbe family puts us in touch with Dr. Escolar in Pittsburgh.
- **February 16:** Dr. Escolar asks us to come to Pittsburgh the following day to see how far the disease has progressed so they can determine if Tori is a stem-cell transplant candidate.
- **February 17–21:** Lesa, Tori, and Lesa's parents take the train to Pittsburgh and back. Many tests are performed and it is determined that Tori is already in stage three, so she is not a stem-cell candidate.
- **February 27:** Tori has an appointment with pediatric surgery to discuss the G tube and Nissen procedures. We also have an appointment with the Hummingbird Program to start discussing

comfort care and other ways they can support us through this process.

- **March 2:** Lesa and Brennan decide that it is best for Tori to have both the G tube and the Nissen. Surgery is scheduled for March 23.
- **March 4:** Early Intervention comes to meet Tori and Lesa and to gather information. The first evaluation is scheduled.
- **March 23:** The G tube and Nissen procedures are performed, and we are in the hospital for two days.
- **June 5:** Tori begins to lose the ability to swallow; the suction machine soon enters our lives.
- **July:** We attend Hunter's Hope Symposium, create Tori's bucket list, and celebrate Tori's first birthday!
- **November:** We take our quarterly trip to Pittsburgh and come home on oxygen.
- **December 8–13:** Tori is hospitalized for five days for low sodium levels.
- **December 25:** Tori's second Christmas.
- **February 15, 2016:** Blue episodes begin and increase in frequency.
- **March 17:** Our trip to California is cancelled and my parents decide to fly out for a New England road trip.
- **March 26:** We arrive home and Tori has her worst blue episode yet, but recovers.
- **March 27:** Tori enters the gates of heaven, Krabbe-free.

A Letter to the Parents Whose Child Was Just Diagnosed with Krabbe

Like most pain, until you have known it for yourself, you are blind to it.
—SARA HAGERTY, *EVERY BITTER THING IS SWEET* (P. 20)

Dear beloved parents,

Everything is going to be okay.

I know you are terrified and heartbroken right now. You got a great deal of bad news in one day and you now know two things for sure: your baby is dying, and given the genetic risk, you probably shouldn't have more children.

That's a lot for anyone to process.

Today you heard the word Krabbe for the first time and you already hate it. The disease is going to rob your child of vital functions, and there's nothing you can do to stop it.

Take a deep breath and allow yourself to grieve. Your world has just been turned upside down, and you don't have to pretend that everything is okay, that you are okay.

But don't let the grief overwhelm and overtake you. Not yet.

Your baby is still alive, still aware, still fighting. Hold her tightly and cherish each precious moment you have with her. Remember that Krabbe hasn't taken full hold of her yet, so take this opportunity to LIVE with her. Choose to find joy each day and appreciate the days you are given. Create a list of experiences you want her to have. Take photos every day and don't take anything for granted. You don't want to have very many regrets when she is gone, so live life abundantly now!

Allow others to help you with the day-to-day tasks, with meals, with finances. Be humble and gracious and receive what others wish to give. They feel as helpless as you do, and they only want to help.

Contact Dr. Maria Escolar (Children's Hospital of Pittsburgh) or Dr. Joanne Kurtzberg (Duke University) immediately—they are experts in Krabbe/leukodystrophies and will help make your child's quality of life so great. Their teams are amazing and will be an incredible resource for you.

Soon enough your home will be filled with medical equipment. The gentle whirring of machines will become commonplace. The daily care of your child will become more complicated as time passes. Don't dwell on this, but be mindful of what the future holds.

Krabbe is terrible. There's no doubt about that. But it is often treatable. You will learn all too quickly that your child could have received life-saving treatment if it had been caught at birth, before the symptoms showed up. But instead of simmering in anger, prepare to join the fight to have Krabbe added to each state's newborn screenings when you are ready to do so. It won't save your child's life, but it will save the lives of others.

Connect with the Krabbe Community—they will quickly become your family and they will be your greatest support. Allow them to speak wisdom into your life. Allow them to walk this road alongside you.

You will find that Krabbe and other leukodystrophies aren't so rare, after all, but the incredible love and support you will receive from those walking a similar path is. We're a family forced together by a tragic disease, and we make the most of our circumstances.

For now, focus on love. On life. On your precious child who was born for a greater purpose. Don't worry about what you can't change, but instead fight to make your child's life the best it can possibly be. And know that we—the Krabbe Community—are here for you, every step of the way.

About the Author

Lesa Brackbill is a California native and Azusa Pacific University alumna who courageously followed the Lord's leading and moved to Central Pennsylvania when she was twenty-five years old. There she met her husband, Brennan, and *Even So, Joy* is their story. Lesa and Brennan live in Hershey, Pennsylvania, and are expecting Krabbe-free identical twin boys in April. Their daughter, Tori, is Lesa's inspiration, and she writes to encourage others and increase awareness about Krabbe leukodystrophy. Visit Lesa's blog and website at www.thebrackbills.com.

Printed in the United States
By Bookmasters

Printed in the United States
By Bookmasters